Why Oracles Are Silent

Why Oracles
Are
Silent

by

Tom Gelinske

Writers Club Press
New York   Lincoln   Shanghai

Why Oracles Are Silent

Writers Club Press
an imprint of iUniverse, Inc.

For information address:
iUniverse
2021 Pine Lake Road, Suite 100
Lincoln, NE 68512
www.iuniverse.com

ISBN: 1-58348-397-7 (Pbk)
ISBN: 0-595-74472-9 (Cloth)

Printed in the United States of America

For my Storm,

Without whose
love, help and inspiration,
none of this would have happened.

CONTENTS

CHAPTER I. ANCIENT ROOTS...1

The discovery of the spirit or soul within us happened not suddenly but by degrees. The discovery of our humanity was followed soon after by a parallel awareness of an individual spiritual destiny.

THE GREEKS 3

CHAPTER II. SPIRITUAL POWER 15

The notion we have of the presence of a spirit within us that is distinct from all manifestations of our physical being is perhaps the only 'proof' of its actual existence. Some people need much reassurance on the question of the presence of this spirit: others simply take its existence for granted.

CHAPTER III. THE ORPHIC VISION 23

Before we can hope to learn of ancient oracles with any empathy, understanding or even comprehension we must first be initiated.

THE MYSTERIES 25

CHAPTER IV. OUR ORPHIC HERITAGE 39

Not all these religions harbor oracles, but in all there will be found a faith that something beyond that which is known can be known, and that history can be read in both directions.

THE BATTLEFIELD OF THE SPIRIT 41

CHAPTER V. THE ORACLES 51

In the religious age communion and communication between Earth and Heaven and Heaven and Earth seemed taken for granted, not just in Greece but in Jerusalem and Babylon and Egyptian Thebes as well.

TALKING TO THE GODS 53

ORACLES IN HISTORY 57
THE ORACLE AT DELPHI 61
THE ORACLE OF MOPSUS...71
THE ORACLE OF AMPHIARAUS 72
THE ORACLE OF ASCLEPIUS 73
THE ORACLE AT TEGYRAE 74
THE ORACLE OF TROPHONIUS 74
THE ORACLE OF APIS 76

CHAPTER VI. THE ROMANS..77
THE SIBYL 79
BIRDS OF OMEN...81

CHAPTER VII. THE CHRISTIAN WORLD....................................85
NOSTRADAMUS–THE LAST ORACLE?................................87

CHAPTER VIII. HOW TO START YOUR OWN RELIGION 95
THE SPIRIT FREED 97

NOTES BY THE WAY 107

I.

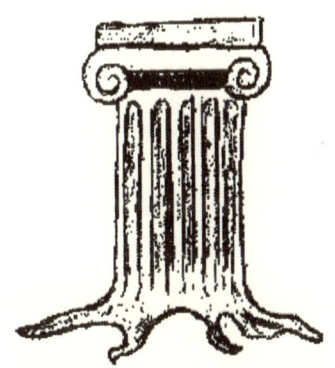

ANCIENT
ROOTS

For those who lack the inner wisdom,
there is no knowledge of whence we come,or
whither we go; such know only what is at the
moment.

—*Baghavad Gita*

THE GREEKS

It seems necessary before setting out on our journey to the world of ancient oracles to look first at some fundamental considerations pertaining to both the particular customs and beliefs of the people who regularly consulted oracles, and the universal human spirit that has always prompted our curiosity about future events. The differences between groups of people, whether race to race or age to age, are far less important than the similarities. (With individuals however, the opposite may be true.) Still, as different as the world was 2,500 years ago, human beings were quite the same. The difference now as then is one of worldly situation…the material plane. The human spirit is the mortar that binds all ages, all races, all humans.

Yet we still have difficulty in our grasp of and our description of this timeless essence of us, with whence it came and whither it goes, what it is, therefore, and why. Is it soul? Is it mind? Is the spirit inclusive of intellect? Is the way we use our brain sufficient proof of the existence of a spirit that motivates us to be what we call human?

And is the spirit immortal? Is 'spirit' coterminous with 'soul?' These questions are asked in quite different ways from culture to culture, which is to say that there is inexorably a kind of cultural evolution, though we use the term advisedly, for this evolution should in no way be confused with progress. We must try to look at it objectively, pragmatically, to account for differences in the way humans deal with ideas, and hopefully enlarge thereby our own horizons. Cultures change. This is obvious at any given moment in history looking from place to place, as well as through time, and attests to the variegated ways in which we humans approach basic and similar situations.

The discovery of a spirit or soul within us happened not suddenly but by degrees, and well before the 10th millennium, BC….or the 20th…or the 30th. Perhaps farther back than that. Once the idea dawned on the human that it was the only one who had a thought, was like nothing else in creation, was simply capable of being bowled over by the miracle of existence and the mystery of death. Once the idea of immortality occurred to him…that is, right after the foreknowledge of his own death…he embraced immortality. It was a matter of

3

choice. In effect what it is to be human, by comparison with everything else, is to be god-like, to possess what no other creature has...a conception of Eternity.

We may speculate too that the discovery of our humanity was followed soon after by a parallel awareness of an individual spiritual destiny. The entity 'spirit' or 'soul,' as distinct from yet part of us, a puzzlement, non-spatial, immaterial but nonetheless existent, even if perhaps but a felt certainty supporting a statement of faith. Whether or not the concept is true, be it inspiration or self-deception, the idea of a spirit that motivates our corporosity had...and has...cosmic consequences.

Still, ideas, even the most basic, take time to mature. Ultimately, in the West, the felt awareness of 'spirit' as a uniquely human attribute resulted in the most remarkable fluorescence of human thought, endeavor and success ever!

As we see exampled around the Mediterranean by the first and second millennia this was not simply a religious awakening or anything that can be done en masse like pyramid building, but was the result of an awareness of essential human qualities such as memory, foresight, abstract thought...for, coupled with those individual differences in these areas, to go back to beginnings, the assertion of identity brought about a self-awareness which led to the notion of individuality, and from thence to the recognition of traits not at all material by which the individual may be described.

If we say for instance that so-and-so is 'clever' we would be hard put to demonstrate that assertion simply by pointing him out. The evidence must be found in some action on his part which was the result of his mental process. 'So-and-so' therefore may be described in totally non-physical terms; he is distinguishable by virtue of a mental trait. That makes him different, but he is not alone. Everyone in the tribe may be so described...that is, in terms other than physical, yet each as an individual with differentiating attributes...as 'happy,' 'pessimistic,' 'optimistic,' and as either sharing opinions or not sharing them. In a trice we are assigning not only personality as an independent trait all humans share, but the implication of a spirit that motivates and colors our 'personality,' our 'individuality,' our 'mind.'

Human self-discovery was but the first of man's fundamental, cosmic discoveries, but it was the one that changed everything, and made possible all that followed!

As we were and are we have come up from survival by means of the idea of individual spirit, and the creativity resulting from this acceptance of something called mind, soul or spirit as being shared individually but without exception, led to the natural, human intellectual competition which by the time of the Greeks, the principle and primal influence upon our own civilization, allowed them to leave barbarism, and with the help of their overweening faith in human destiny, to develop a culture which was not just another anthill but a model for ages to follow.

In retrospect, that time and that place seem clinically right for what happened, and even the things that were wrong with it worked to its success, as for instance the Greeks' poetic and polymorphous religion, their pantheon full of unlikely Olympians, the lack of a genuine creator god, any really unifying religious force, which in their case only seemed to push metaphysical speculation into other directions, a lack which was in part at least responsible for the Milesian turn toward the study of the empirical world of sense, and personal involvement in that world of everyday reality...that is, ethics, government, as well as the study of the elements that led to science. The Greeks managed to keep the spiritual and the material each to its own realm, and were confident that all of us partook of both the material and the spiritual in equal portions.

In Greek philosophy arguments about the mystery of existence and the nature of reality led to new avenues of thought, not doctrinaire conclusions which might preclude further speculation. One needs only to glance at the Middle Ages to see how the best minds of Europe went wasted in their universal preoccupation with scripture, a bad habit finally broken only by heresy and internal dissent.

The Mediterranean was the great sea in the middle of the world, surrounded by Spain, France, Italy, Greece, the Hellespont, feeding and floating also on the Black Sea and its ports, Odessa, Colchis, the mouths of the Danube and the Don, the trading towns along the Ionian Coast, Ephesus, Rhodes, Cyprus, Asia Minor, Tyre and Sidon, Egypt, North Africa, Carthage, Crete, Sicily. The time and place were right for a high form of civilization to develop or evolve, and one is tempted to put forth all manner of theories to account for how and why it came about, only to become swamped by all the good reasons.

The Mediterranean was a buoyant highway over which to float ideas, and early on Egypt exported hers to Crete along with the trade goods, and spreading them further along the African coast to Carthage were the Phoenicians, those hardy sailors, who planted Marseilles some 4500 years ago, who circumnavigated Africa about 665 BC, who introduced the Greeks to the alphabet, and taught them the intricacies and virtues of sea-borne commerce. The Greeks learned from the Phoenicians as they did from everyone. The fundamental nature of

Hellenic civilization was derived from the Minoans of Crete and combined with the incursions of Northerners into Greece, who were themselves swallowed by the civilization they found there, by its language and its gods, and left behind their barbaric ways. They mixed and then, centuries later, as Greeks, as Hellenes, they moved outward, conquered Crete, destroyed Ilium (Troy), colonized the Black Sea, and traded from there to Egypt, to the Pillars of Hercules, even the Canaries, Italy and the rest. The Southern part of Italy was colonized, as was the eastern shore of Sicily, not by one country it must be noted, but by one culture.

The Mediterranean (as a broad highway of commerce) was in effect 'discovered,' first by the Phoenicians and Minoans, then by the Greeks, and it was a discovery as revolutionary in that era as the printing press or wireless would be much later. Whatever happened in any port fronting the water was soon known in every other port, and as far inland, presumably, as one could walk with an oar on his shoulder before someone asked him what that was. Ideas spread on the wings of news, and that was the principle export of the Greeks, who in that regard it must be said, were borrowing as much as lending; but everything went through the mill of the Greek mind.

From the point of view of history this rush of greatness took many centuries. The beginnings of self-awareness or identification as Hellene begins about the time of Homer, but perhaps not yet at the time of the events depicted in his epic 'documentary,' *Iliad*, Homer provides the fanfare, the pantheon and the manners (the social rules) as the curtain opens on the Hellenic phenomenon. Hesiod contributes also heavily to the society's view of itself. Taking the year 800 BC as a beginning and seeing its peak at 400 BC, the decline of Greece was as slow as the rise. It is significant that by the 1st century Greek was the language in which Christian scripture was written, the language of choice, it being seen as more necessary to be understood than to remain with the 'holy' Hebrew or Aramaic. Around the Mediterranean…from Jerusalem to the Pillars of Hercules the Greek language (the dialect koine) was used the way English is used today around the world as the language of commerce and air travel (you can't have babble in the tower) as the language most likely to be spoken and understood. The writings of old and new religions were painstakingly preserved in Greek, which had not only the capacity for precision but the poetry necessary to convey spiritual ideas.

By 400 BC Athens was at the center of a commercial, artistic and intellectual universe, and it is no accident that this political, philosophical greatness coincides with its economic greatness. Yet practically at the same moment it became engaged in a war with Sparta in its attempt to retain its empire. Athens lost the war, and was afflicted by a plague as well which tragically foreshadowed its decline. We are not trying here to represent Greece as some politically perfect Arcadia. Utopias are obliged to exist in time, like flowers, and must decay and go their way.

Even at its best in Greece, tyrants still usurped, there were perversions of justice...as in the trial of Socrates. Sometimes bad triumphed over good, and the Greeks as we have seen weren't unanimous about anything. There is no evidence they thought they were ushering in a Utopian age...in spite of Plato's Republic (which was after all intended as nothing more than an intellectual construct, a philosophical exercise which attempts to seek out a definition of 'justice'). On the contrary the Greeks were still too close to the barbarity of the past, and surrounded by it, to entertain any fiction that they had all the answers: but they were hot on the trail of independent human thought and endeavor when the rest were prostrate before some deity or other which was supposed to solve all their problems by miracle and intervention, in exchange for slavish and unquestioning belief.

The Greek was on his feet when the rest of the world was on its knees. He was already too independent to put his complete faith in anthropomorphic gods, even the ones he had himself invented...yet without any diminution of his belief in the spiritual side of life. He still believed in his gods, and propitiated them, still took seriously signs, sibyls and omens...was indeed pious by any standard, on average much more so than we in the modern age. And this piety extended beyond mere propitiation and sacrifice, beyond fear. In a country that could barely support the small population strictly maintained by each city-state, in a country that bred Spartans, the Greeks learned to revere and not fear what was lofty, fine, divine, and they had the notion that what is truly real and truly immortal is what is inside our heads.

> ...he who has been earnest in the love of knowledge and of
> true wisdom, and has exercised his intellect more than any
> other part of him, must have thoughts immortal and divine,
> if he attain truth, and insofar as human nature is capable of
> sharing in immortality, he must altogether be immortal...
>   —Plato

Plato attributes divinity to truth, and thereby sanctifies the intellect. Here he notes the oneness with spirit that can be attained by use of the mind. The wise man and the saint are in close relation.

They philosophized in wonder, 'in order to know, and not for any utilitarian reason,' Aristotle tells us, proposing a more worldly description of the virtues of thought. In effect there existed a 'think tank' in Athens, and in the love of their own creation...civilization...they felt they could afford their sophists, as they could afford their art, music and poetry, which also have no 'utility.' It was a sign of their distance from barbarity and mere survival. As things turned out however, philosophy proved very useful...this sitting around chatting, playing volleyball with ideas, logic and language, as well as freely engaging in the independent contemplation of seemingly useless notions...such as Democritus' atomic theory, for instance, or the elements of Empedocles...entirely metaphysical ideas at the time, having nothing to do with empirical reality.

Nonetheless, their non-utilitarian approach to thinking is still paying off. By this method the Greeks learned how to think, and they passed on their discoveries to us in the disciplines of logic, grammar and scientific objectivity. They discovered (for want of a better term) the universal nature of mathematics and geometry, the importance of method...and they came to believe that such knowledge, even wisdom, was accessible to all regardless of circumstance, gender or station, that it imparted a certainty to the grasp of the workings of nature which could be counted on...and all this...as it turns out for us...proved practical and was a boon to succeeding ages, starting as it did from non-utilitarian contemplation, thought for its own sake, what is...ungratefully...sneered at today as 'ivory tower,' though it is essential to an understanding of who we are and how we got here.

The Greeks recorded monumental gains in the annals of intellectual progress as the result of their belief in the presence in humans of a spirit within, of a soul that partakes of and is identified by intellect and individual personality, the existence of which is universal and provable, however non-material, by its effects. And if the mind or spirit could do this...solve problems, pose conundrums, philosophize, be understood by other minds, there might be no limit, they felt sincerely, even beyond infinity and eternity, to the mind's ultimate capacity to understand. The non-material part of our being...soul, spirit or mind...might travel beyond this universe, explore new realities...and through time travel even from one existence, one life to another, explore the very regions of Heaven and Hell.

The Greeks were fearless without being foolish, courageous at all events, and they accepted in this wise both life and death, with the proud assertion of their humanity in their ready acceptance of what is true and certain, as well as in their unstinting pursuit of what is yet to be known!

What is known to the spirit can become known to the mind, if one is but an aspect of the other. And this too is a statement of faith that leads to an infinite however unknown universe of adventure and discovery. The Greeks believed that universal ideas are innate...that which is naturally and universally known, as well as true...and that the mind innately recognizes the truth with little prompting. The mind therefore has a window on the truth, upon the universe and therefore upon things yet unknown, truths yet to be discovered, worlds beyond our own, realms of the spirit too. Their investigation of the elemental and empirical world in the objective and secular fashion they studied it in no way precluded belief in the spiritual side of existence or in religion. It is refreshing even today to read Herodotus for the respect he invariably shows for the multitude of religions he met in his travels in Persia and Egypt (5thC. BC). Although Herodotus loves a good story his *History* betrays the objective, receptive attitude of the true journalist.

The European university system is based on the classical Greek and Latin body of discovered knowledge, and its works and methods of instruction, which is to say it is the seed of our own education; and the way in which this learning is imparted was modeled upon and took its inspiration from that effulgent outpouring of collective intellectual and creative genius that seems, especially now, incredible, even miraculous. This tradition has been interrupted in recent years by technology and events so that now, for instance, one need not know Greek to be considered well-educated (a college fad that goes back to Roman times), or need to be conversant with the 'classics' or know who Aeneas was, or Democritus, though we still cultivate nodding acquaintances with Plato and maybe Pericles, Solon or Aristotle. However, these minds still exert their influence, still inform the way we think about things, yet more and more unconsciously.

We are no longer required to recite the catechism of philosophy in our classrooms. Now few know the distinction between formal and final cause, or the parable of the cave. If we do learn these things it's because we have a personal interest in the foundation of our cultural edifice, an interest in how and when our ways of thinking in the Western World took the shape they still retain, as in logic, rhetoric, mathematics, geometry, the importance of history in our thinking as the study of the past useful to our own present. The Greeks bequeathed to us objectivity, the secular view, the empirical science of Thales and Democritus, the mathematics of Pythagoras, the engineering genius of Archimedes, the aesthetic dimension, ideas of moderation, democracy, individual liberty, fair play, scientific observation and experimentation, the language of science, medicine, pharmacy, atomic theory, politics, physics, psychology…all these are part of our thinking, whether we are aware of their roots or not.

The Greeks didn't invent all these things; the items on this extensive list didn't come about all at once like things and people in a creation story. The Greeks didn't invent any of them, strictly speaking…they discovered them. All invention is a rearrangement of discoveries about the world and how it works. Yet not all invention (as we see with the Greeks) is the child of necessity; sometimes it is the result of native creativity, intellectual inspiration, and sheer mental playfulness, as in for instance the atoms of Democritus. Why would anyone in the ancient world we may fairly ask set about looking for anything like the smallest indivisible particle of matter…and that as an explanation of the building blocks of all perceived material reality, as an explanation of the nature of existence? Even as a belief this metaphysical description of the world has no practical result. So that particular idea had to wait 24 centuries before bobbing again to the historical surface. No doubt the Greeks will continue to prove their parentage in ways yet to be known, providing more surprises about ourselves and what we know, reminding us that people didn't suddenly become smart a century or so ago, and that our own intellectual roots go back to a tiny country in the Mediterranean, with little to export but ideas and olive oil.

The Greeks were from their first arrival on the scene a kind of switchboard, centrally located as they were for the job, as much as they moved about influencing and being influenced. Being as imaginative and creative as they were everything they found and used they improved upon, from ships to government, from coinage to the alphabet. As a habit of mind they examined everything; being competitive they tried to go it one better. They not only competed with everyone else they were most competitive with each other...a trait which has its negative side to be sure...but strife is natural to competition, and competition is necessary to progress, and progress they did...far beyond their non-Greek neighbors, not that these were not outstanding themselves: the Persians, Egyptians and Phoenicians, yet Greece rose in this milieu to an excellence pre-eminent in human endeavor, surpassing even those who later surpassed them in power, like Macedonia or the Romans, who conquered in admiration, even reverence.

Early in the 1st millennium new and vital civilizations, with their attendant strife and invention, were growing up throughout the world from Greece to China, and all in roughly the same period. The older societies like the Babylonians and Egyptians were giving way to the Persian Empire, which dangerously rubbed elbows with the Mediterranean civilizations. And given the rate at which ideas travel the similarities between the Greeks and the people, say, of the Indus Valley or Babylon are not surprising. It is perhaps more surprising that the Greeks and the other societies around the Mediterranean found themselves in a more accelerated rate of progress, and in Athens we find the most cosmopolitan, sophisticated city of all in a place and period of the most intense social, intellectual, artistic and commercial advancement. That is the place to which brains and talent always gravitate, which only swells the talent pool, and stiffens the competition. At its peak (after the Persian Wars of the 5th century) Athens found itself creating an empire almost in spite of any intention.

These amazing people, our intellectual forefathers, gave us also the concept of culture, defined as a principle, as a social goal and need, as describing a conscious striving after aesthetic and intellectual excellence. Today we apply the term 'culture' rather indiscriminately to all societies as a description. It was in effect a process of iconizing concepts such as 'the Good' quite apart from either religion or utility. For the Greeks 'culture' had everything to do with what still seems ineffable to us, and we call 'class,' which doesn't capture it, or 'taste,' which is only a part of it, or 'sophistication,' 'education,' 'breeding,' or all these together, and we would have only a halting and partial description altogether of what the Greeks themselves called simply *paideia*. Centuries later the artful Florentines used the word *'virtu'* trying to encapsulate in their love of classical antiquity one of its most elusive yet pervasive ideas, applying it to itself. At that the Florentines had excellent innings.

The rise of Greece, and its eminence in the Mediterranean world, the energy with which its notions of culture, individuality, moderation, democracy, influenced the world around it all have everything to do with the self and the power of the spirit. It is the same impulse of spirit that motivated the rest of the religious age, though in Greece, as the result of a rather fanciful cosmogony and a plethora in their pantheon, unity of faith suffered, and the individuality of their selves and their *polei* suggested delicious alternatives. And they were not content to keep their ideas to themselves. The Greeks by the way seem to be the most peripatetic of the ancients...witness the travels of Pythagoras, Plato, Xenophanes, Herodotus, Solon and many others (with the means to do so, of course)...they seem to be the first tourists. All roads lead both ways. So they brought ideas home, and of course disseminated their own abroad. The miracle and mystery of existence did not elude their attention, and the first dim wonderings over the idea of the purpose of it all can lead the sanest and most reasonable among us to pose some kind of Deity whom we might represent as having that purpose. But when everyone else was rushing to the safe harbor of some doctrinaire cult or religion, the Greeks plied the unknown seas of spiritual adventure; they explored freely all the regions that could be imagined or could be thought of, without agreeing or settling on any one idea as the truth and the whole truth.

The Greeks also have had free and untrammeled choice and selection in all areas of belief, and no fear of oppression from without or within. It would have seemed too outlandish (barbaric) for a government to oppress individuals for their beliefs. We can find no guarantees of religious freedom in anyone's constitution...none were needed and therefore none were expressed.

The Greeks were probably the most sophisticated people (as such) who ever existed. They invented things before the things were needed! Machinery, atoms, metaphysics, geometry, etc. They did not deride any investigation into the supernatural, the metaphysical, the mental, the spiritual or the religious. Free inquiry reigned there too, and whether or not they believed in such stories as Orpheus' adventures in the Underworld, they certainly grasped the metaphorical message contained in such tales. And while they grasped the parabolic nature of the stories told by poets and priests, they could suppose gods who inhabit an Olympus, or imagine a personality which is the individual spirit travelling beyond this life to realms yet unknown, even to Hades, where only souls of the dead abide. The Greeks, worldly and shrewd as they were, could yet imagine not only the transmigration of souls, but reincarnation as well, as part of a personalized and individual destiny for each of us.

Because the Greeks were as clever and as secular as they were, they were not bound as most people were and still are to pass on their superstitions, prejudices, doctrines and philosophies to their children as dogmatic truth. The spirit of free enquiry was not squelched in the nursery. What beliefs individuals arrived at were not the result of being led to conclusions before the reasoning power was fully developed. This attitude led to a full flowering of individual imagination and creativity. They were not afraid to think beyond their own science and philosophy.

They dared to imagine, therefore, the possibility that the future could be known. The gods were not subject to time and could read history in both directions, and through augurs, sibyls and oracles this kind of divine knowledge could also be made accessible to mortals.

They thought about time. Out of Chaos arose Kronos (Time) who paired with Rhea or Geia the Earth Mother (Matter), to create reality (the World). Before this pairing all is chaos; from it all else follows. Time and space are inextricably married, but they are not the same thing. Immanuel Kant in the 18th century promulgated the idea that time and space are simply forms of reality, and thus made science possible. However categories forestall investigation. Once the idea is neatly explained we can stop thinking about it and move on. But wait a minute. Is the explanation sufficient and satisfactory? It may be a disservice to enquiry to dismiss time as a mere form. It may be as bad to speak of it as the 'fourth dimension,' for that puts it in the same category as space or matter; but we know that the latter actually fit into the former and not the reverse. Time may be said to have two dimensions of its own: the future and the past. Time is its own unique form, and as such it remains an enigma, an undiscovered country. Time cannot be taken for granted, as no less a mind than Albert Einstein knew full well, whose lucubrations on the subject open up whole new avenues for discovery. So it is with the fiction writers, daring in thought, like H.G.Wells (also a historian), who construct time machines in thought, and future worlds in potentiality.

The Greeks, too, unencumbered by hard and fast dogma, were also free to contemplate the possibilities. Having begun to see things in a historical perspective, as events occurring in time and affecting events to follow, that acts have consequences, and by simple logic much may be deduced about the future. It is no great leap to imagine one who may have a gift for divination...and perhaps knows how to seek divine help. The roads were filled, from Galilee to the banks of Tiber, with those who claimed such knowledge...bakkids sibyls, prophets, seers, and the like, preaching the doctrine of the spirit, describing realms beyond the here and beyond the now, laying claim to foresight, to arcane forms of knowledge gathered by them in their journeys through the realms of religion, of philosophy, of the soul and of the spirit. Some of their teachings crystallized into religions like the Eleusinian and the Orphic mysteries, and the office of prophet or oracle became familiar and pervasive enough throughout the culture that shrines were created, temples erected, so the people would know where to go, and knowledge of future events could be, they felt, virtually as certain as water from the well.

By the classical age, Greece was dotted with oracular shrines, the most famous of which is at Delphi, which became rich beyond imagining, a far cry from the itinerant preachers and prophets, who had traveled the roads, begging their bread, during the migrations. The oracular tradition seems to go back as far as Orpheus, who along with his other attributes wrote the first oracular poems, and preached a doctrine of the spirit and its transmigrations which was the fountainhead of many religions to follow, down to the modern age.

II.

SPIRITUAL POWER

...we are luminous beings. We are perceivers.
We are an awareness; we are not objects; we
have no solidity. We are boundless. The world
of objects and solidity is a way of making our
passage on Earth convenient.

—*don Juan Matus*

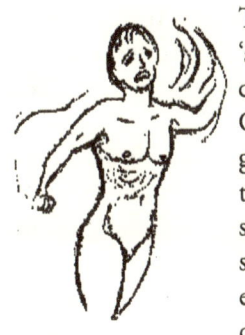The spiritual world of ancient belief has been 'swamped'...to use Carlos Castaneda's term...by the success of modern science and civilization. This must include Christianity, since the institutionalized and sectarian religions of today bear little resemblance to the original spiritual faith of the followers of Jesus. Islam may be still a survivor among the modern believers in that faith, yet the symptoms of desperation among its most devoted followers betray their own feeling that in the face of world change, even the days of Islam as a spiritual system are numbered. Quite naturally the Faithful feel deeply threatened by the Western World: the very existence of its technology cuts spiritually deeper even than the certainty of military defeat by its overwhelming material power. What's more, we can imagine that the religions of the West are seen as hypocrisy by Moslems, and a manifest contradiction.

Was Bismark right? Is God on the side of those with the biggest guns? In the ancient world the difference between armies was the difference between the men, their discipline, will, determination and motivation; in the modern world the difference is between the technologies, the size of the guns, the industrial might of one side or the other, and renders the human equation as of little account.

The empirical fact rears its adamant and terrifying aspect. It is a juggernaut, dominating the terrain, changing the scenery, overcoming all resistance, as inescapable as Fate. Once established it creates its own direction, follows out the logic of its own implications, and rides roughshod...with iron boots as the proverb has it...over all who fall in its road, crushing the spirit too, more than ever famine, general war, plague, pestilence and death itself could ever ravage at their absolute worst.

There are only remnants, a few survivors of the wars, wandering off to look for others of their persuasion, a motley few who refuse to accept the facts, banding together in cults of one description or another...poets and prophets, both unheard and unsung, evangelists, savants, fortune tellers and astrologers. As in politics, the religions of today make strange bedfellows. There is a closer emotional connection between the Evangelical Baptist, say, and the Zionist, or between Jerusalem and the Vatican, now that all beliefs are threatened by the facts. At the time of the crusades, the Jews traveled with Islam, in tandem as it were, and they got along quite well together...against the threats of Christianity toward both. Jewish scholars in their travels with Islam during its spread kept alive the works of the classical Greek philosophers, like Plato and Aristotle, when European Christendom in an attitude more of hostility than neglect sought nothing less than the complete eradication of the memory of such Pagans and their heretical beliefs.

The notion we have of the presence of a spirit within us that is distinct from all manifestations of our physical being is perhaps the only 'proof' of its actual existence. Some people need much reassurance on the question of the presence of this spirit: others simply take its existence for granted, as Catholics for instance take for a given that they have a 'soul.' Less spiritual but still rationalist intellectuals retain in their lexicon something called 'mind'…itself dismissed by the logical positivists, epiphenomenalists and others of their materialist persuasion.

The spirit is for some the entity Descartes was attempting to demonstrate and illustrate as the 'I am,' the spirit or soul within the core of individual identity as the fundamental existential certainty we have of our own reality, as in fact the ultimate certainty, the kernel of truth upon which the rest of the world…nay, the universe…is built, as the key to any hope of knowing anything at all about that universe! The spirit is that which is not material, as in the impulse to religion, the appreciation of art!, the felt need for a metaphysical reality existing behind life's appearances, the need for order and design. Some need the assurance that the world and existence make up some kind of understandable entity. Love in the best sense has everything to do with the spirit, as do the belief in notions like honor, or liberty. All belong in everyday ways to the idea of the spirit…both patriotism and revolution, the search or simply the longing for what's good…God, philosophy, intellect itself. And to what realm do we ascribe creativity, talent, or genius? We may even speak of good and evil as related to the health or sickness of the spirit. And the term 'spiritless' may be applied to an individual or to an entire society.

The German philosopher Hegel said that human speech is the only medium capable of conveying ideas such as spirit, and it may be that human speech was at the root of belief in such things as spirit and religion. (This is not to call the notion of spirit into question. Our becoming aware of something is not a prerequisite of the reality of its existence, Bishop Berkeley to the contrary.) Since one hand washes the other, speech, and its resultant language, suggest to the mind possibilities not immediately seen, mental constructs…language becomes more than mere communication: it becomes a tool for thought. 'True' and 'false' are as valuable terms and as practical and useful as 'right' and 'left'. Thus language becomes more than saying 'Time to put the cows out to pasture,' or 'Don't drop that!'

The spirit in its turn suggests immortality, by its nature, independent as it seems to be at the outset from the material world of birth, death and appearances. Even Lucretius…Epicurean, pagan, atheist…believed in reincarnation, insisting however that the transmigrating spirit suffers a kind of amnesia in its passage from one life to the next.

Since the spirit is by definition not material it is not subject to the rules of mortality, to birth, decay and death. The idea of mortality suggests immortality. From society to society and era to era the belief in some sort of re-incarnation, in Heaven, or Valhalla, or perhaps a personal roost a step higher on the wheel of life, or with our ancestors…all persist with an almost universal longing and faith; yet with the exception perhaps of the ancient Egyptians, no one ever thought of taking the body along.

You tell 'em and you tell 'em! You can't get to Heaven in a rocket ship! Or on the tail of anybody's comet!

The spiritual is not the material.

Nonetheless the power of the belief in the individual soul or spirit is and always has been undeniable, palpable in its manifestations. Some historians of the ancient world credit its belief as instrumental in the institution of law and the state's primacy in its execution. Originally murder, for instance, was a matter concerning only the families of those involved. If a member of my family is killed, it is up to me to kill the killer. Then one of theirs will come looking for me, etc. But not all families are powerful enough to exact retribution, and when they are, it only leads to feuding and internecine strife. In the former case the family might go to the tribal or clan leader and ask for recourse, and their complaint might well be that "the souls of the dead cry out for vengeance." They are being haunted in effect by their murdered relative, who won't leave them alone, who won't let them sleep until some recompense is made, some revenge exacted. Not only did the leaders of the tribe see the virtue of this argument, it also behooved them to take over the function of naming penalties and exacting retribution, as necessary to the public peace, to forestall endless feuds. The argument of restless spirits also introduced a religious element into the argument, so the city, state or tribe was able to declare a crime such as murder an abomination or pollution on the city, which could only be made clean once more in the eyes of the gods when the scales of justice had been balanced.

Such is the power of belief, and those who believe attribute some powers to the spirit which are not dependent upon the material person having departed this world. Great minds indeed have held these opinions of the power of the soul or spirit.

> O, my friend, how prophetic is the human soul.
>
> Socrates, in Plato's *Phaedrus*, 242C

> O, my prophetic soul!
>
> *Hamlet*, Act I, sc.v.

In young Hamlet's utterance on hearing from his father's ghost that Hamlet's uncle Claudius was his father's murderer, the prince is saying "I knew it!" And that is a common enough expression for us all to understand what it means. Hamlet's foreknowledge of the truth is however no more provable in law than the word of a ghost on a battlement, and his inability to act upon his knowledge (!) or to have an entire faith in it marks him as the first truly modern hero in drama. The clash between spiritual certainty and material necessity is certainly spotlighted in Hamlet. And as there is nothing new under the sun, Shakespeare virtually cribbed the line from Plato. And Socrates' utterance shows much more conviction about its truth. The prophecy hidden in each human soul or spirit, itself wrapped in the opaque cocoon of material concerns, cries out for release, yet this form of knowledge is today, in our modern culture, stifled in the crib. It was not so for Socrates.

Plutarch maintains that the soul or spirit in its pure form...as *daimon*...reads the book of time forwards and backwards, unencumbered by corporeal imperfections, mundane confusion or physical obstruction. The spirit that we possess, locked up within our worldly form is in contrary case, blinded by material necessity and all the rest. We possess the original power of the spirit within us, yet in an inferior form. Tied to the material, we grope through a dark landscape of mere appearance and illusion. Moreover, according to Plutarch:

> The faculty [of the spirit] will be either weak and faint, or slow and laborious, like seeing through fog or moving through water.

and:

> ...it [the spirit] will need much care in the healing and reviving of its *native* force...(italics mine)

Plutarch adds a happy image to his argument:

> The sun doesn't *become* bright when it emerges from clouds;
> it always *is* bright. (italics his)

Plutarch believed that the spirit is indestructible, and that, freed from the 'present,' it sees with an absolute clarity in every direction. The spirit is the essence of us, though we see in this life as through a glass darkly, as St. Paul might grudgingly agree. Plutarch considers memory and prophecy then as corresponding faculties. The past, Plutarch argues, is as immaterial as the future, so the soul has the power to see both ways, though the future, he concedes may not be so clear, yet the awareness possessed by the soul often blazes forth 'in dreams,' when that aspect of the self is dissociated from any daily reality, freed of its mundane fetters, like the convict (I speak from experience), who dreams his way to freedom, aided by the very darkness and solitariness of his deep confinement, in the hole, even in the jail within the jail, where yet the soul breaths out "alone at last." The rules are left in another place and time, for:

> The prophetic tablet of the mind has no writing on it, no
> rational sense, no definition provided by itself.

In the modern world there are few (outside of one or two artists) who would agree with what Plutarch has uttered here. Yet at times this second century writer seems as modern as any avant garde poet or painter or musician. Even in his own time an opinion like this made a maverick of him.

Plutarch seems to be a writer's writer[1]. He is a sincere Orphic and a priest of the Delphic shrine. His dialogues don't rank with Plato's, but they are literate, learned and entertaining, and in many ways as descriptive of the times as a newspaper, but mostly his original work is concerned with spiritual values.

But before we go any deeper into this question of our spiritual nature and its prophetic capacities, we had better spend a few words on the topic of Orpheus and the Orphic mysteries.

---

[1] Consider what Shakespeare owed to Plutarch: **four** stories! ...Coriolanus, Julius Caesar, Antony & Cleopatra, Timon of Athens, and endless inspiration too, no doubt, and reams of useful information on the times, the customs and the style of thought.

III.

THE ORPHIC VISION

My soul is tossed about in the whirl of the elements—
air, earth, fire and water...from one to another, a
wanderer banished by God.

—Purifications, Empedocles

THE MYSTERIES

Before we can hope to learn of ancient oracles with any empathy, understanding or even comprehension we must first be initiated in the "mysteries." They are of two kinds, the Eleusinian and the Orphic. We will be concerned mainly with the latter. Imagine that we could return to the second millennium BC, to an entirely undeveloped northern Greece.

We will follow a pilgrim, we'll call him Nomius, who walks from Larisa in Thessaly some two or three hundred miles, through Macedonia to Thrace. Nomius is a religious man, he has consulted the oracle at Dodona and asked there certain questions about life and death. The priest has advised him to journey to Thrace, to seek out a man called Orpheus.

Nomius sets out on his pilgrimage. He must live on what he can beg along the way. He doesn't worry about being robbed. Money hasn't been invented yet. Since his pilgrimage is religious, he will be taken in and fed by those who share his piety. There are no roads, no inns, only rude and rocky pathways up and down the mountains. Nomius must depend upon the honest directions of the locals, his only passport being the fact that he shares language as well as religion with the people he meets. There is a kind of miracle in his journey, in the 13th century BC, given the natural isolation of towns and people, separated by rugged mountains, rushing rivers and uncharted seas. Our pilgrim must travel on foot, perhaps preferring the coast for a good part of the journey as not so much up and down. Through the wildness of Macedonia he treks (8 centuries or so before King Philip and his son Alexander gave the place a name).

The land becomes wilder and more overgrown as the pilgrim approaches Thrace. From conversations he has had along the way he knows the person he seeks is not far away, in Doriscus, beside the River Hebrus.

Nomius has heard marvelous tales of the Thracian Prince Orpheus, who some say is half god, who in his earlier days had lived a life of adventure and romance, had traveled with Jason and the Argonauts in search of the golden fleece, was said to play the lyre with such charm the birds and animals would approach him unafraid; and when the sirens who lay in wait for unwary travelers heard his mag-

ical notes they forgot their own, and enraptured, allowed him and the Argo to
pass.

Nomius was told too how Orpheus had followed his wife Eurydice down to
the Underworld, but had returned without her. The fact that he had returned at
all amazed the pilgrim. And yes, of course Nomius believed what he heard, just
as the pilgrim to Jerusalem a couple of millennia later believed he had a chance
of bringing home a piece of the true cross.

Prince Orpheus was said to have not only the gifts of music and poetry, but
of prophecy as well. Nomius has heard all this, but what attracts him is this new
teaching of Orpheus concerning the spirit, that the spirit is in all of us. It was all
second hand, what Nomius had heard, but it intrigued him, as much as he
understood of it, and he wanted to hear more from the master himself. He had
been told that Orpheus preached that we all partake of a spirit that makes us
immortal as any god, a spirit that travels through time from one life to the next,
sloughing off the old life as a snake does last year's skin.

Nomius has heard all this and more about this demi-god, half human, half
divine, that he has oracular powers, composes prophetic poetry...and his followers collect these poetic and oracular utterances as items of the faith. Orpheus
has also forbidden blood sacrifice or any killing of animals, and this is a sore
point to many who have been long habituated to offering up lambs, goats and
oxen in propitiation. For Orpheus however the doctrine of the transmigration of
souls means that these souls may in their journey from one life to the next
inhabit the bodies of animals. Thus in killing the lamb one might well be mur-
dering a relative; at the very least, a natural and holy process is being traduced in
hastening any death.

What Nomius had heard seemed to make sense to him, for he had often felt
spiritual longings and questions of a similar sort, and when he contemplated the
vast star-scattered heavens that looked down, Nomius had the restless thought
that there was surely more to creation than his house, his family, his village. He
wondered what it was that made him what he was. Was he but a traveler through
the world?

He had many such vague but nagging questions and these had at last led him
on this quest, and as he drew closer to his destination, Nomius fell in more and
more with other pilgrims, who told him more wonderful stories of Orpheus.
Nomius wondered just how much of all he had heard could be true. Orpheus
certainly must have a profound effect on people to set into motion such tales.
Mostly Orpheus prophesied, in lyrics set to music of rare and heavenly notes, in

a voice magnificently charming and hypnotic. The more he heard the more anxious Nomius was to see and hear Orpheus for himself. The demi-god preached and sang of the retribution of a divine justice and the promise of an ultimate Heaven, the ultimate abode of worthy spirits.

Nomius then heard that Orpheus was in the next town. At last he was approaching the object of his curiosity and wonder. The poet-prophet had arrived only the day before, in a flower-strewn parade of his followers. Nomius was told this by someone who claimed to have been a part of it.

But then Orpheus had interrupted the sacrifices that were being made to Dionysus Zagreus on this festival day. One must picture the scene correctly. There were no temples yet. Most gathering places of worship were in a glade perhaps, the central piece of furniture being a large stone sacrificial altar, an offering thereon, and a priest with a knife. There would also be a fire, a pyre of sorts, upon which the ox, lamb or goat would be roasted. It was very much a barbecue picnic put on by the church. In strictly hungry human terms it must have been that. Thanks to Prometheus' blessed trickery, the gods were only interested in the bones and the fat…and of course in the fragrance which rose up to their domains. The humans feasted on the rest. In the event, just as the ceremony of the sacrifice was going smoothly, Orpheus had appeared. There was a disturbance, some sort of riot ensued, and this man had hurriedly left the scene. Now Nomius began to worry, but the man could tell him no more.

Then someone else came along from the direction of Nomius' intended destination, this time an old man wearing a very hang-dog expression.

"What is it?" Nomius asked him. There were others too coming along the path, sad, distracted, staring off as if in shock.

The old man Nomius had stopped rubbed his eyes as if waking from a dream. "We were sacrificing to Zagreus and Orpheus came along and forbade us to kill the ox we had prepared with garlands and libations. The priest was about to use his sacrificial knife, and it was just then that Orpheus leaped upon the altar and told the priest to cut his throat instead. You'd have thought it was a human sacrifice we had laid out there.

"Well as usual, the very sound of his voice had us all in his sway—all except for a few maenads, already drunk with unwatered wine. They ran off rather than listen to the words of the master.

"The rest of us sat down to listen to Orpheus speak in that wonderful voice of his…but before very long the drunken maenads returned, beating on drums and blowing sour notes on the pipes, making every kind of din, so that they could not hear and be charmed by Orpheus' words. When they got close enough they attacked him with knives and sharp swords, rending his body in pieces, arms, legs all cut and torn from the trunk, and finally his head! This they cut off and cast into the river." The man looked at Nomius tearfully. "Some who saw, say that the head was singing, singing, as it floated down to the sea."

And with that, we leave our pilgrim. I apologize for the way this story ends, but it reflects my own disappointment at arriving too late. In my case about 3,200 years. It's hard to know much about anyone who lived that long ago. What is amazing about Orpheus is the endurance and persistence of his influence and ideas.

When Orpheus descended into the underworld (the first time) there was little known of its shadowy precincts. The demi-god gave our world its first reports  on the terrain, so Shakespeare was mistaken when he called it "the undiscovered country from whose bourne no traveler returns." It was Orpheus, according to ancient tradition, who mapped out the territory. Orpheus was the son of Calliope, one of the nine muses, and King Oeagrus of Thrace, who some say was a river god. Apollo gave young Orpheus a lyre, which the muses taught the child to play so well that he could charm not only men and beasts with his musical magic but move rocks and trees as well. With his lyre and his voice he could rearrange the scenery. We have already told how Orpheus journeyed with Jason and the Argonauts when they went to seek the golden fleece, and with the power of his music got them out of many a scrape, as when he charmed the sirens into silent admiration.

Orpheus' best-known adventure was his descent into the underworld to rescue his wife Eurydice, who had been bitten by a poisonous serpent. Orpheus in his descent used his music to charm Charon into carrying him across the River Styx on his one-way ferryboat; then Cerberus, the fierce 3-headed dog who guarded the gate to Hades, was soothed and quieted by Orpheus' lyre.

There are a multitude of variations in the story from this point on. One is that Pluto wanted Eurydice for his own wife (which would account for the snakebite, the snake being a creature who lives underground, and is as we will see with the Python, magical in itself, a messenger and minion from another world).

In some versions of the tale, Orpheus charms Pluto with his music, in others Orpheus must match wits with Pluto. This takes a variety of forms, sometimes a game (one of the most interesting versions being that suggested in a modern film version of the tale, *Last Year at Marienbad*, in which the Pluto or Satan figure lures Orpheus into a game which he, the Lord of the Underworld, can lose, but never loses).

In the event, Orpheus is allowed to lead Eurydice out of the Pit, provided he does not look back to see if she follows. He does look back, and loses her forever. Monteverdi uses this scene in his opera *Orfeo* with stunning effect. Near the entrance to the World with all its sorrows, tribulation and noise, and "half in love with easeful Death," Eurydice begins to nag at Orpheus till he turns to look at her and when at last he does she promptly disappears back to the quiet and shadowy domain of Pluto. In many later versions, Orpheus upon his regaining the upper world again is torn to pieces by the maenads. His head, thrown into the river, floats, still singing, down to the sea.

Virgil, Dante, Monteverdi, Gluck, Byron, Poe, Shaw, Renais, Cocteau, Tennessee Williams, and legions of poets here unnamed fell under the spell of the story of Orpheus. And much has been said and written on that score, but the religious and spiritual significance of Orpheus' writings, where we can divine their content from secondary sources, show an influence as pervasive in the faiths that followed—those of Zarathustra, Buddha, Krishna, Mithra, Jesus, Mani and Muhammed, to name a few.

Speaking as we have of our own ancient roots, the writings and the teachings of Orpheus appear to be the root and seed of many religions, East and West. Orpheus, if he was a genuine historical figure, was more than morale officer in Jason's *Argo*, more than a magical minstrel, and was not simply the father of all poets and musicians but of saints, martyrs and prophets as well!

We must interpose here and remind the reader again that all we know of Orpheus and his teaching has come to us second hand, and yet it does constitute a most intelligible body of religious thought, and given the quality of thinkers (Plato, Empedocles, Heraclitus, etc.) who have passed on to us what are called Orphic ideas, odds are good that the basic outline of the religion was the gift of one mind.

It is not strange that we have no fragment of Orpheus' music or poetry, but only the example of his "character and deeds," as Plutarch might put it, as an inspiration to succeeding generations of poets and prophets down to our own time. Plato was aware of writings on religion attributed to Orpheus, as in his dialogue "Cratylus," where he has Socrates quote Orpheus, literally and authoritatively, but from what source we do not know, since these writings have not survived.

Orpheus, as distant as was his prehistoric time, may indeed have been a genuine, not a fictional, personage. It is difficult to escape such an assumption, given the manifest effect and influence of Orpheus upon all poetry, music and religion to follow. No mean feat for an obscure Thracian of dubious godhead, and we will try to demonstrate these claims hereafter, as yet another example of Greek "firstness" and profound originality.

By the time of classical Athens, in the 5th C. BC, Greek culture was shot through with rich veins of Orphic belief. The mysteries were well received, particularly in the cities. The physicist Empedocles wrote Orphic poetry as well as metaphysics. In *The Purifications* Empedocles writes:

> My soul is tossed about in the whirl of the elements—
> air, earth, fire and water...from one to another, a wanderer
> banished by God.

Empedocles added that the soul must journey a mystical path, out of the miserable cycle of the process of the elements to which it is bound in the material world...up toward the pure and divine realm once inhabited by the original soul. It seems obvious that as well as being one of the first "scientists," Empedocles also followed the Orphic way, and was inspired by the doctrines he found contained in Orpheus's own poetry.

Heraclitus believed in the soul, and he resolved the problem of its co-existence with the material by reasoning that the soul survives the coming-to-be and passing-away of all material things in the universe by virtue of the soul's kinship with the everliving fire of the cosmos...for the soul has the capacity, Heraclitus believed, of knowing divine wisdom within itself. To the soul, in other words, the idea of eternity is self-evident.

Well before the 6th century BC bakkids and sibyls walked the roads of Greece preaching Orphic ideas, such as that of an individual's possessing an everlasting spirit that would inhabit a hereafter; and in their teachings, these Orphic wanderers described the next world. During this period they collected the utterances of oracles and this collection might indeed have constituted the beginnings of a written text. The trouble is that the religion dates back beyond the beginnings of writing, back through an oral tradition, perhaps thousands of years before the Bible or any of the events depicted therein.

The more common religion of the centuries between, say, Homer and Archimedes, was that of the Eleusinian Mysteries, a bucolic, straightforward set of beliefs, based mainly on ideas of fertility, regeneration and the simple mystery of the seasons, withal a rural and straightforward faith which reflected a pastoral existence. The Orphic mysteries seemed to have been more acceptable within city walls…a way for citizens perhaps to find escape, however momentarily, from civic stress. Orphism is closer to Dionysus than to Demeter, more sophisticated in its view, however poetic, spiritual and ecstatic its approach.

A brief and further comparison illustrates another difference, and some similarities. The principle player in the Eleusinian mysteries is Demeter, who searches for her daughter Persephone, herself in the clutches of Pluto, Lord of Hades and brother of Zeus. In the Greek world Demeter is a different kind of hero. In her gender she embodies the idea, or ideal, if you will, of mother. She is the personification of fertility, maternal concern, and female ingenuity. Demeter searches long, and only after much travail discovers where her daughter is being held. Demeter goes to Zeus and informs him that nothing on Earth will grow until her daughter is returned to her! No crops, no fruit, no flower will grow or blossom, there will be no grass for the sheep. Zeus prevails on Pluto and a compromise is reached wherein Persephone must spend 3 months of the year with Pluto. These correspond to winter, when nothing bears fruit. The pomegranate, a late autumn fruit, is associated with Persephone.

The Greek Pantheon is evenly divided among six gods and six goddesses. Zeus, male warrior-god is Chief, and Athena his daughter, born in full panoply of war, usually votes with the males, but that may only serve further to explain why the men are on top socially. The legend of Theseus conquering the Amazons and taking its queen Hippolyta to wife may be more than an explanation, and may indicate that there was in Greece in the distant past a sizeable state ruled by women, who also did the fighting. True or false the legend demonstrates a Greek readiness to explore all varieties of human existence and social interaction. It illustrates, as does the potency of goddesses like Demeter and Athena, much about the status of women. There was no proscription of women who wished to belong to the Eleusinian or Orphic religions. All were admitted to either, if they chose to become initiates. One could belong to both.

Slaves were admitted without condition to these religions. The mystery religions were, on the logic of their own belief, against the practice and institution of slavery. Humanity is what it is regardless of circumstances, and whatever is mortal is possessed of a spirit, they believed, that is immortal. The mystery religions introduced a note of fundamental equality, the beginnings of democracy.

The Orphic religion was but one among many of the same sort that gathered currency before fading into the back pages of history. Mithraic cults, the Rites of Isis, Serapis…all flourished in the religious era. The multiplication of religions followed the same road as the variety of deities required to cover the needs of the congregation. Orphism seems however another Greek 'first' in its promulgation of the basic tenets of spiritual belief, and for this reason we are obliged here to look further into its mysteries.

Rules and rites must be followed by the faithful. Initiates may not be admitted to the tabernacle without purification, just as for instance in Catholicism today confession and penance precede communion. It could be fatal to the soul to arrive in an unclean state. With proper respect the votary desires release from the worldly and the mundane, oneness with the object of its spiritual longings.

The Orphic Religion had its mundane prohibitions; one must not eat beans, one must not poke fire with iron, one must not eat meat, or be buried in woolen garments.

Paramount in the teachings of the Orphic Religion is the identification of the individual spirit with immortal attributes as well as longings. The spirit is destined to journey beyond the world, beyond the present, beyond time and space, proclaiming:

> I am the child of Earth and the starry Heaven.
> I too am become god.

But only by following the rules and rites of the religion will one's everlasting spirit be released from the Weary Wheel of continuous incarnation before arriving at Heaven's recognition and admittance. The promise is explicit.

> Happy and blessed one, thou shalt be god instead
> of mortal.

Yet in the process of ascending to a final release from the Weary Wheel one may go through several incarnations. Hence the prohibition against eating the flesh of animals. The idea of reincarnation wasn't generally believed in Greece, as witness the general practice of sacrifice. But an Orphic would have regarded killing and eating of animals as possible murder and cannibalism, for any kind of being might be a relative, be it fly, dog or T-bone steak, and such an act would put the spirit of the offender in jeopardy of descending down, not up, the ladder of existence, longer to serve on the wheel.

Was Orpheus in any way an historical personage? In a fragment handed down to us, Empedocles, an Orphic, speaking of an ancient people mentions that

> ...there was among them a man of unusual knowledge, and master especially of all sorts of wise deeds, who in truth possessed greatest wealth of mind; for whenever he reached out with all his mind, easily he beheld each one of all the things that are, even for ten and twenty generations of men.

If indeed he is speaking of Orpheus, Empedocles in the fifth century is speaking of someone at least six centuries earlier (20+ generations), and that might put this "man of unusual knowledge" right in Jason's boat.

Empedocles, in another fragment, speaks admiringly of a particular religious sect, dedicated to Cypris (Aphrodite).

> "Having rejected other gods, only her they worshipped with hallowed offerings, with painted figures, and perfumes of skillfully made odor, and sacrifices of unmixed myrrh and fragrant frankincense, casting on the ground libations from tawny bees. And her altar was not moistened with pure blood of bulls; for it was [they felt] the greatest defilement among men, to deprive animals of life and to eat their goodly bodies."

It is interesting that this unknown religion was dedicated to Aphrodite, still it is typically Orphic in spirit, not that that would be a contradiction. What we know for sure is that the Orphic religion is based on a form of worship that long precedes the 10th century in Thrace. It was a Dionysiac cult, a more civilized form perhaps of earlier local rites which among many others was being accommodated to Hellenic culture as it developed through the early half of the first millennium. As Greek culture flowered the Hellenic world engulfed local religions through the commonality of language. Forms of government as always remained a matter of local preference, whether monarchy, oligarchy, democracy or tyranny. (In its early use this last term referred simply to emergent leadership.)

Pisistratus, an early king or tyrant of Athens, introduced the Orphic religion to the city-state, and for a time the Orphic rites and teaching had wide appeal, but then were reduced to the status of a cult, perhaps because of the discovery of the corruption of one Onomacritus, a poet, who altered certain prophecies for his own use and advancement.

Still the essence of Orphic beliefs persisted in the best minds of the era following. Orphic doctrine differed from the mainline of popular belief. Again we may be reminded, the Orphic mysteries began as a local Thracian religion that persisted in its own peculiar practices. Religions like people each have their own personality. Although Orphism springs from Dionysiac roots, it teaches more Apolline virtues, such as moderation, artfulness, and vision beyond the immediate, that led to the idea of wisdom (as forethought), as well as to the notion of reading (seeing) history both past and future.

It's possible Orpheus was torn to pieces because he was a reformer who civilized more ancient and barbaric Thracian rites. The maenads (the conservative element) in their frenzy tore him to pieces perhaps because he forbade human sacrifice, or any kind of sacrifice or eating of meat. The Apolline moderation Orpheus taught was at odds with the older Dionysian barbarism of Thrace, and proved his mortal undoing at least, at the hands of flesh-eating extremists.

> Robed in pure white I have borne me clean From man's vile
> birth and coffined clay, And exiled from my lips always The
> touch of meat where life has been.

Such is Euripides' version of an Orphic hymn.

From another fragment we find a description of the entrance to the other world.

> Thou shalt find on the left of the House of Hades a well-
> spring, And by the side thereof standing a white cypress. To
> this well-spring come not near. For thou shalt find another
> by the Lake of Memory: Cold water flowing forth, Guardians
> stand before it...

This fragment like so many others is just that, a teeny chunk from the past, one of those out-of-context hunks of poetry, history or wisdom that only makes the scholar thirst for more. Thrace is an outpost of Hellenism, and its door fronts on Asia, which might account for differences again with the mainline, as in the Orphic account of Creation. Time (Kronos) lays an egg and out of it is hatched Eros-Phanes, primal god of love and light, who creates everything...Heaven and Earth and presumably the gods themselves. Zeus swallows Eros-Phanes and from his original creation brings a new world (the one we know) into being.

When the Titans slew Dionysus and devoured him, Zeus in revenge slew the Titans with a thunderbolt…and from the sooty residue of his divine fire a race of humans was born, a race which partakes of both the earthly (Titanic) and the divine (Dionysiac) elements, these are the children "of Earth and of the starry Heaven."

Carnal and spiritual: the first needs to be controlled, the second cultivated. We can see the Greek exposition of these ideas again in the Greek theater, and therein too we can see that the ideal and the influence of Orphism is not holding some drunken revel around a fire, or occult and forbidden sacrifice by the dark of the moon, as Hollywood might depict it; on the contrary the Greek theater exploits the divinity of music and poetry and the profound effect they have upon the spirit; it functions as a temple of the soul, and thereby fulfills the Orphic promise. Purgation of evil was its stated goal, the cleansing of the soul. Just as the ceremony of the church has drama, so Greek drama contained the deepest questions of piety. The fusion of religion and art is the most basic of Orphic ideas. Plays like *Oedipus Rex* which highlight a moral code, define behavior, and outline the do's and don'ts in the *polis* on pain of Heaven's displeasure, exerted moral leverage just as did the story of Job for the tribes of Israel. In Greece as practically nowhere else, religion inspired poetry and made its intimate connection thereby to beauty, to the aesthetic in support of religion, brethren as they are at the same feast of the spirit.

The Orphic mysteries, while not for everyone, demonstrate a belief in a spirit that springs from divine roots, an individual spirit which will in time return to that exalted state of ultimate release and freedom. In a very serious sense our walking about on the Earth is like Orpheus' descent into the underworld.

In his *History*, Herodotus, with his usual ingenuousness, tells the story of Aristeas, an Orphic poet. Aristeas had the habit of disappearing and then turning up in odd places. One day Aristeas walked into a shop in Proconnesus and quite unexpectedly dropped dead. The shopkeeper, in an understandable state of anxiety—Aristeas' family was among the most prominent in the town…hastened forthwith to inform the relatives, but when he did, he was contradicted by a houseguest who averred that he had met Aristeas on his way to Cyzicus, as he, the houseguest was on his journey here, so Aristeas could not have been in town at the time the shopkeeper said Aristeas died in his shop. The family nevertheless went into town, to the shop, but there was no Aristeas, no dead man to be found, there or anywhere.

Seven years later Aristeas showed up without explanation, and stayed in Proconnesus long enough to write a poem famous to the Greeks as the *Arismapeia,*
then he vanished again. Three hundred and forty years later Aristeas turned up
in Italy, practically the other side of the world. The Metapontines, who were
Greek colonists, reported that Aristeas appeared in their midst and told them
that they were the only Greeks in Italy, and that Apollo had visited them. The
poet knew this for he had followed the god, flying after him, Aristeas at the time
being a crow (presumably in one of his many incarnations). Now Aristeas com-
manded the Metapontines to build an altar to Apollo, and a statue to himself.
Then Aristeas disappeared again.

The Metapontines sent to Delphi to ask what they should do, and the Pythia
told them they had better do as they were told and build the statue. And so they
did. Such was the credence in these things, and the power of the Orphic reputation; for after all, Orpheus is the grandfather of all oracles, the god-father of all
prophets.

We're going to these lengths about the Orphic mysteries…and Orphic
poets…to illustrate by demonstration the pervasive influence of this religion,
through Greek culture to our own. Its messiah, Orpheus, whether god or man at
the beginning, through poetry, music and oracular prophecy is also the god-
priest of the cult, come down to serve mankind, and to be at last the martyr if
you will, the intercessor with Eternity, the anointed one, the *christos*…through
art and philosophy as well as religion, everything about this religion aims at exalt-
ing the spirit. The life…and death…of Orpheus was the inspiration to the congregation, which you may be sure contained a healthy contingent of poets,
musicians, philosophers, teachers, mathematicians. The congregation of the
faithful…geometers and playwrights, pan-pipers and statesmen, stoics, cynics
and skeptics, even those self-styled atheists, the Epicureans, who nonetheless
believed in reincarnation, all of them looking for something good, all seeking
within the Orphic mysteries the regeneration of the spirit…proclaiming therefore the spirit as a thing unquestioned, however variant the definition.

The influence of Orpheus continues millennia beyond the remembered precepts of the cult. The Orphic inspiration is just that. The manifest intention is
to in-spirit the faithful, to awaken the divine half of their human nature, and to
inspire them in a positive way, toward the spiritual, away from the mundane. The
world is always with us; it is the spiritual, the Heaven within us, that we must
seek.

Most religions are outgrowths of attempts to understand what's happening, sprung from the desire to solve certain mysteries, those of life and death or good and evil, the nature of nature or the nature of the universe, where do we come from and where do we go. There are perhaps as many explanations as there are questions, which may make it all seem strange that those resulting beliefs are put forth each with equal fervor, spread with the sword, if need be.

Nowhere, except for the Brahmins of India were a people more religiously tolerant than in Greece. Generally there existed a policy of accommodation of the variations of practice and belief from Italiot Greece to the Pontis, though the accommodation was not always peaceably put into place, as we will see. In fact the history of spirit religions from the first prophet, Orpheus, has been from the outset a battlefield. The conflict is practically the foundation of the metaphysics.

IV.

OUR ORPHIC HERITAGE

'Tu se morta, se morta, mia vita ed io respiro—'[2]

—Monteverdi

[2] "You are dead—dead, my darling, And I live…"

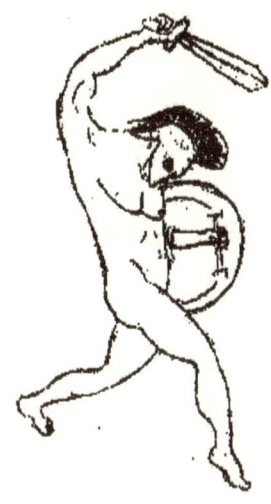

THE BATTLEFIELD
OF THE SPIRIT

We can see when we look into the life of someone like Pythagoras that the spiritual appeal of Orphism was particularly strong within the intellectual as well as the poetic spheres. Pisistratus was welcoming the Orphic religion to Athens at about the same time that Pythagoras introduced the Orphic Mysteries as a state religion in the city of Crotona in Italiot Greece.

The Orphic religion had great and widespread appeal, at least for a time, and it seems its cosmogony made some kind of geometric sense to philosophers and mathematicians such as Pythagoras, just as the romantic story of Orpheus' descent into the Underworld had great panache for poets, dramatists, scenarists and musicians.

Pythagoras, the Greek philosopher and mathematician, was born in Samos in the 6th century B.C. He left his homeland and traveled to Media where he is reported to have sat at the feet of Zarathustra. It may be more likely that they had a commonality of views about many things, perhaps most particularly the spiritual side of existence. Pythagoras, as a Greek, was already steeped in the Orphic mysteries, and he undoubtedly saw in Zarathustra's teaching a deep Orphic strain. Its primal god was one of light, Ahura Mazda. God himself is the Cosmic Design; God is the role of the spirit. Certainly, in all its abstraction Zoroastrianism must have appealed mightily to the patronymical ancestor of all mathematicians.

Unlike the Orphics, with their scattered oracular poetry, the Zoroastrians had a book, or set of books, called the *Zend Avesta*, the Book of Knowledge and Wisdom. The God of the religion was the heavens, or the very idea of Heaven. This is the first clue to the abstract nature of Zorastrian teachings. Its notions of 'mind' and other non-material abstractions must also have appealed to Pythagoras.

The common following of Zoroastrianism tended to personify the qualities and ideas of the doctrine, such as 'light' or 'piety' into divine personages, a habit picked up from polytheistic religions. But Pythagoras would have been content with the abstract notions he found in Zarathustra's teaching, being himself in search of cosmic designs, immutable laws and mathematical certainties (however divinely inspired) by which his geometrical thinking might arrive at truth.

The teachings of Zarathustra were ultimately incorporated into Persian religion through the Magi, those priestly princes, and Zarathustra was counted as one of their number[3]. The bowdlerizing of Zarathustra's teachings was necessary to its success. For. even at first glance, these precepts are as we say abstract and quite difficult, and should be clearly labeled NOT FOR EVERYONE[4].

Returning to Greece and ultimately migrating to Crotona on the Italian peninsula, Pythagoras became involved in the government of that Greek colony, gained political power, and introduced the Orphic religion as the state religion. The first to call himself 'philosopher,' Pythagoras became master of a school of philosophy which held that the rules of the universe, of geometry and music, and indeed all things else, were as sacred as they were immutable and certain. Order, design and meaning are deified in Pythagoras' doctrines. Apparently he attempted to re-design government itself along more religious lines. It was probably a crucial error to mix religion (however geometrical) and politics. In any event the experiment failed...as many years later Plato failed to make a Republic of Syracuse according to rational and philosophical principles.

Whether the Greeks feared state religions (i.e. the mixing of politics with religion) or the Orphic religion itself occasioned the reaction, the shrines and temples of Orpheus were desecrated and its followers persecuted soon after the failure of Pythagoras and the downfall of the state religion he fostered. Into Athens as we mentioned in the same period Pisistratus welcomed the Orphic religion, where its mysteries found popularity for a time, and indeed the cult took its first roots in Attica and spread from this fertile ground.

The virtual disappearance of the Orphic religions of Greece still left in its wake a body of spiritual influence upon poets and philosophers, still left traces of belief in the intuitive forces and longings within people striving in their way to know the ineffable. I wanted to be the first to say this, but I read in Gilbert Murray's *Five Stages of Greek Religion* the observation that in the failure of the Greek religions to survive history, they nonetheless handed to following generations a body of poetry and drama, created in the love and spirit of those old beliefs, art of a beauty and quality far exceeding the aesthetic inspiration provided by most other and still accepted religions.

---

[3] Interesting, that it was these Magi who visited the infant Jesus, bringing gifts and thereby conferring approval of "the annointed one."

[4] In contrast, Jesus never confused heart with brain, and in his direct appeal to the simplest of his flock, fostered a religion for all the people, and seemingly for all time-for those who most need a religion.

The Orphic mysteries themselves gave in early to the practical hard way of the world, to Stoicism, Cynicism and Epicureanism in philosophy, and to the practical application of geometry. Perhaps one does need a world rather like that depicted on the vase in Keats' 'Ode on a Grecian Urn,' an ideal environment, an Arcadia where one goes to slake one's spiritual thirst and forget the contumely of the present and the material.

An American philosopher, maybe it was Santayana, once said that in any contest between the strenuous and the genial, the strenuous will drive the genial to the wall. It is perhaps also true that material exigencies will always drive out spiritual considerations. Christianity of course is full of contradictions to that observation, almost stock-in-trade if you will, the incidents of spirit overcoming material, usually of course to the fatal detriment of the material. Yet the irresistible force of the material is seen as helpless in the face of the spiritual. But all of that for the individual is dependent on a belief in the survival of the spirit in some realm beyond and only suggested by the material, a proposition not provable to those who dwell exclusively within the confines of the material. Belief in spirit, however indefensible it may be, seems to persist, and in this way our interest in the spirit survives any questionable instance.

The variety of human experience is such that the belief in God is far from universal...that is belief in a creator God, a jealous or all-powerful God embodying in Himself all positive virtues, etc., God with a capital 'G.' In the ancient world that notion of God was confined to a small tribe out on the desert. It's quite a handful of virtues for the gods of most civilizations. It's not odd that at first glance Greek religion little resembles Christianity, Islam or Judaism. When you think of the thousands of deities of India, Persia, Assyria, Sumeria, Babylonia, when you think of Baal and Krishna and Vishnu and Brahma and Kali, Horus, Isis, Osiris and Mithra, you're hard put to find similarities. But when you believe that ideas travel on roads and faster than people, you find yourself looking out for the basic strain that runs true through all variations.

Werner Jaeger, a modern and highly respected scholar says of Orpheus,

> "He gave them the mysteries and taught them to abstain from murder."

He tells us too that the Orphic doctrine of the soul "was the beginning of a new consciousness of the self and a new feeling for human life[5]." This was indeed the beginning of something!

---

[5]In *Paideas*

The Orphic teaching was a prelude to a new perspective that humans were gaining upon themselves. Orpheus was most probably a gifted prophet or preacher of some distant century of the second millennium in Thrace. Perhaps he was a prince, if not a demi-god as legend suggests. He was likely a poet and teacher of great power and taught his following the doctrine of metempsychosis, or the transmigration of spirits. He taught that the soul is our best part, that it only inhabits or uses this body as a tardy and rather inefficient means of conveyance through the world. The spiritual being is in fact a sojourner and guest in the world (yet the journey through any present existence is itself part of the process of purification). This belief entailed the prohibition of blood sacrifice or even the eating of meat, which meant that participation in the sacrifice, a long-practiced religious ritual, was forbidden in the Orphic sect.

Although Orphic belief was essentially a refining of the older and less controlled Dionysiac religion, in his proscription of blood sacrifice Orpheus went against the mainline of Hellenic belief, and was perhaps martyred by the more violent and sanguine forces of opposition, perhaps (like Jesus, and others) because he was a danger to the status quo.

Orpheus is a demi-god, and this means that though he is sprung from the divine, he must die a mortal death. As Toynbee and others have pointed out, the figure of the demi-god appears again and again in the 'Book of Humanity,' in the figure of some half-human half-god who suffers for his commitment and service to mankind and must die (or be exiled from the world) because of the jealous wrath of some more powerful god or by the tragic misunderstanding of an ignorant humanity. The shape of the story has to look something like this, and does, from Orpheus to Jesus, including (Toynbee tells us) Zagreus (it means 'torn to pieces'), Tammuz, Attis, Balder, Adonis, Husayn...and later on, Mani, the founder of Manicheism, a form of Zoroastrianism/Orphism, a dualistic doctrine, again the battle between good and evil. This Mani was crucified and his body flayed for upsetting the powers of his day, in 277 AD.

Zarathustra was said to have been consumed in a flash of lightning...the story had to end that way, since Zarathustra, like Jeremiah, outlived any martyrdom and barely escaped deification. Deification is important but not necessary in the Orphic story. Again Toynbee quotes, this time Isaiah: "For God so loved the world, that he gave his only begotten son..." and thus godhead is conferred upon the martyr, if it wasn't already assumed that he was sprung from the divine, as in Orpheus' case.

Orpheus appears as a prophet, divinely inspired, as a Jesus, or a Krishna, or if you will, a Socrates, except that he preceded all of these martyrs to the advancement of spiritual belief. Again, we discover that the pioneer is a Greek. I can't find anyone who precedes Orpheus. He appears to be the fountain and precursor of all spiritual religions. So we will refer to all of these religions as Orphic. Plato's dualistic philosophy also qualifies. That is why even that pagan philosopher finds his thinking acceptable in a Christian world. Or Judaism. Or Islam. What they have in common is faith in the idea of a spirit which travels through time, unbound by any particular life-span, which transcends any limitations imposed by mortal sensation, which understands everything and is able to read the future as easily as the past. That is the legacy of Orpheus and the promise as we see of Christianity, Islam, Judaism and many others.

The world-wide dissemination of Orphic religious ideas may, I think, be attributed to Zarathustra, at whose feet Pythagoras as we said was reputed to have sat perhaps in the 6th century BC. Pythagoras is a misty enough personage…Zarathustra is even less biographically specific. We know that he taught a kind of dualism of light and dark, good and evil, with Ahura Mazda, god of light as the central figure in the religion, strongly reminiscent of Eros-Phanes in Orphic belief. Yet God Himself is conceived as the heavens themselves, the cosmic design, virtually a principle, though It had adjectives connected to It, and these qualities themselves became personified, in the minds of the followers of the sect. What was an attempt to unify, though a failure, contributed to the elegance of the religion; yet nonetheless an all-powerful deity requires some opposition to prove his strength. God must have his Satan…and soon you're no longer a monotheism. The attempt nonetheless keeps the religion within bounds. We pray to the saints, don't we? And we Catholics seek the intercession of the Mother of Jesus…all deities, these gods and sons and mothers of gods, as much a family of deities as were the Olympians of the Greeks. The ceiling's frescos reveal as well a multitude of demi-gods, archangels, saints and all the rest.

After Orpheus it was Zarathustra who taught the immortality of the spirit, more successfully than he did the virtue of theistic economy. And it is in Zoroastrianism that the battlefield is most prominent as a metaphor of life, which is seen as a stage upon which the struggle between good and evil is waged constantly.

Likewise the individual spirit is also a battlefield, the scene of a struggle. Purity and honesty will lead to everlasting life, but on the way evil spirits conspire to tempt and hinder us, and our guardian angel is our only protection. Again, gods and titans contend, the divine and the worldly. At the end of life the souls of the dead pass over the Sifting Bridge where the evil fall into the chasm of Hell below, and the good make it across to the Abode of Song. Shades of Orpheus!

There was a purgatory too in Zoroastrianism, as well as a final day of judgement, after which all the good souls would live in a world of unending bliss. And this idea of divine retribution can also be traced back to the teachings of the Orphic mysteries.

From Orpheus to Mohammed, they are all inspirational, Orphic religions...from Orpheus to Buddha (there's still no anachronism there), to Krishna (crucified, died, and rose again) to Jesus, (quite the same), Orphic journeys of the spirit, to Mohammed, suspended between Heaven and Earth. But all supply a civilizing influence on their time and place, all represent innovations, which have always been frowned upon and were often costly to their innovators.

Zarathustra's teachings had their moment in the reign of Darius I, but ultimately Zoroastrianism was radically simplified and Zarathustra himself was inducted into the company of the Magi, another individualist co-opted without thanks. Still his ideas (derived from Orphic ones) somehow survived and were picked up by others...that of the sanctity of life, the belief in the spirit, ideas of Heaven and Hell, the eternal battle between good and evil, and a metaphysics encompassing and dependent upon a morality, or at least implying that morality.

Zarathustra was at the center of the dissemination of Orphic ideas, living when and where he did, in Media, which was well named, since it was the halfway station from anywhere to everywhere. If ideas of the spirit and of immortality may be said to derive from Orpheus the Thracian, they were likely disseminated by Zarathustra the Median. From Persepolis all roads led everywhere in the sixth century BC, from and to Egypt and India and Jerusalem and Greece as well.

Zarathustra was another reputed to have more than mortal beginnings, divinely conceived, and at his death (we have already noted) he was consumed in a flash of lightning. He ascended into Heaven, which was partly his own invention. There is no reincarnation taught, but the soul or spirit is no less immortal. Like Judaism and Christianity later the soul at death is judged and ascends into Heaven or is cast into Hell. In consequence sacrifice is not prohibited, as it is in the Orphic mysteries.

Buddha, another Orphic (perhaps through Zarathustra...no anachronism there either), found blood sacrifice abhorrent. Buddhism is said by some to be a theology without a god, but like Zoroastrianism and Orphism it is a philosophy having an intimate connection between its metaphysics and its morality. It sees the world in religious terms, and human behavior is its dominant concern...right conduct. Buddha seems personally not to have believed in the transmigration of souls, but his followers insisted, which indicates that the idea preceded Gautama. The Buddhists, like the Orphics, thought that the quest of the spirit was to end these incarnations in sundry form, that ultimately the spirit would be able to leave the Weary Wheel of existence. One might achieve this by right and appropriate conduct.

Like Zarathustra, Buddha taught something like the Golden Rule, and in this too both anticipated Jesus.

But before Jesus, there was Krishna, heroic deity of the Bhagavad Gita. Of mysterious origins...born in a prison. He performed miraculous cures, restored the dead to life, died...some say...by crucifixion, ascended into Heaven, etc., returned to Earth as the teacher of Arjuna and mouthpiece of the Gita. He taught an acceptance of the world and its tribulation, an immortality of the spirit, and a complete tolerance of all forms of worship.

> Each goeth to that which he worshippeth, according to his degree of spiritual comprehension. Those who worship personal gods or angels, go to dwell with personal gods and angels; those who worship ancestors go to dwell with ancestors; and those who worship spirits go to the land of spirits.
> —Bhagavad Gita

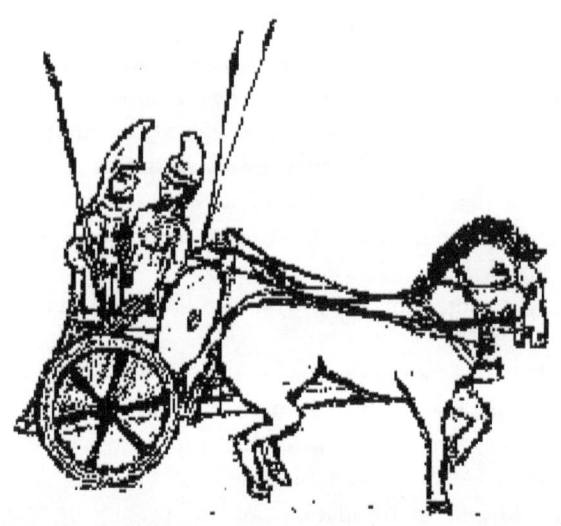

In the Bhagavad Gita the dialogue that comprises the text takes place on a battlefield. Prince Arjuna has his charioteer, Krishna (in mortal form), drive his chariot to a place between the opposing forces, all of whom, on both sides, are members of the same family, drawn up now in battle array, ready for attack and mutual destruction. The prince Arjuna bemoans his fate that he must take part in this deadly, vicious internecine dispute. He has brothers, uncles and cousins facing each other over ground soon to be stained with the blood of all!

The dialogue that follows...the apocalypse always looming...between Krishna and Arjuna, in which Krishna counsels acceptance of the world and its battles, has a dramatic immediacy no writer, ancient or modern, could fail to admire. What is suggested here is the battlefield of the spirit, the struggle, not just between good and evil, but within ourselves, to understand what cannot be understood, to accept what cannot be accepted.

The author of the Bhagavad Gita is not unaware of the grim humor involved in the protracted philosophical discussion taking place on the war chariot, as on both hands must be heard shouts and curses, warlike threats, horses stamping and snorting, their riders impatient for the shock of battle. From a writer's point of view this touch alone...the image of a battlefield, the impending struggle of life and death...invests every word of the dialogue with an immediacy and a meaning unmatched anywhere, in prose, poetry, drama or philosophy.

Krishna, as I say, counsels acceptance, rendering tribute to Caesar, for the world is the world and it is but a testing ground, as it was for Buddha, and for Jesus...and later for Mohammed.

You see the similarities in these stories and the way that the stories are told, the struggle, whether between gods and titans, forces of light and the powers of darkness, or within ourselves, between the divine and the worldly, it is a dualism which cannot be resolved short of Nothingness.

Again and again, through history, they rise, and sometimes preach, and sometimes sing, poets or prophets, individuals who are possessed by the Orphic vision, faithfully following out an idea, a stream of thought, which has everything to do with the stream of time, and our travels through time quite apart from any geography, our travels from reality to reality, underworlds and other worlds. We may become convinced that it is our conception of eternity that makes us human, the persistence of this idea of spirit that connects itself to the *nous*, the cosmic and eternal mind, that insists upon seeing beyond ourselves, our place and our time. The martyrdom of Orpheus only begins a long line of believers in the spirit who will die for the cause, and does not end with Jesus.

I come from the Divine, and to the Divine I shall return.

—The *Sayings of Jesus*, St. Thomas

Not all these religions harbor oracles, but in all there will be found a faith that something beyond that which is known can be known, that history can be read in both directions. And in spite of mortal death we can participate in the future: this faith is found in the idea, as clear and distinct as any self-evident proposition, **that nothing in the universe, whether nuclear or spiritual, can ever be lost.** This, for an Orphic, unlocks the secret of eternal life, for life is a process, one in which we will never cease participating.

V.

THE ORACLES

All roads lead both ways.

TALKING TO THE GODS

In the Religious Age communion and communication between Earth and Heaven and Heaven and Earth seemed taken for granted, not just in Greece but in Jerusalem and Babylon and Egyptian Thebes as well. The Greeks however had their own peculiar and fascinating way of conversing with their deities, and indeed their drama and histories, and we may easily assume their daily lives as well were rich in tradition and belief. Even as their objective and secular view was growing and developing, they still read the entrails of the sacrifice, noted the flights of birds, and took quite seriously dreams, omens and portents. As practical as their needs might be, the attention and intervention of the gods in every facet of life was assumed.

Tales of mythology abounded in oracular warnings, assurances and predictions as motivating elements. It all began with an oracle—the one received by Cronos that his offspring would overthrow him. In the story of the hero Perseus, who slew the gorgon Medusa, the hero's grandfather, Acrisius, received an oracle that his grandson would one day kill him. In his fear, Acrisius set his daughter Danae and her infant son Perseus adrift on the sea in a box, and thereby launched one of the greatest and best known adventures of mythology, at the end of which Perseus returned to his home and in the course of games celebrating the occasion, threw the discus, which the wind carried awry to strike Acrisius the fatal blow.

Even courage was tempered by belief. Pausanias, brave Spartan general that he was, would not advance at the battle of Platea till the auspices turned out favorably, and he had the entrails of the sacrifices read again and again till the portents turned right. Was it lack of courage? I suspect that for the religious Spartan it was simply a matter of timing. The gods were telling him when to go.

Tiresias, blind priest and seer of Sophocles' Theban plays, to return to that for the moment, talked to the birds, who were in their flight close to the heavens and knew the doings and the wishes of the gods. In refusing to believe the bad news delivered by his oracle, Oedipus is obstinate in refusing to accept his own fate, which has already happened to him. But that is no concern of the oracle's. He is only the messenger.

It was the religious age. In that time there was no such thing as accident or coincidence. Reality, seen or unseen, the events within that reality, were a seamless weave. When someone had a dream, it was not simply as if one had a headache…in fact a headache at the wrong time might signify something of concern…an expert in each case must be consulted (as Daniel read Belshazar's dream). And a second opinion might be sought, if the first were deemed unsatisfactory. What all this says, in the large, is that ancient man thought himself in communication with his gods, just as the Christian today seeks communion. From here it seems that the Greeks, and the other ancients, got more answers…or thought they did.

Dreams, too, were a form of communication with the gods, who delivered messages this way, in code to be sure, and subject to interpretation and hope, as Xerxes' dreams before his invasion of Greece, which were tragically (for his armies) misread. (Or sent to mislead him, as a Greek might think.)

'my thoughts fly up…' Claudius at his prayers. (*Hamlet* again.) Like the birds, prayers, wishes, aspirations, are supposed to fly. So too, with dreams: it was imagined that they were a manifestation of the spiritual part of one's being, released in sleep from the cares of the present.

The prediction of the oracle is inescapable, though the truth may be couched in a riddle. Indeed it is always a riddle, but this form invites participation. The receiver of the oracle must take an active part, and interpretation provides this initial modicum of responsibility. The rest of it is up to the receiver as well. You have to do something about it or you have to leave it alone. In *Oedipus Rex* of Sophocles the oracle predicts the death of Laius at the hands of his own son, who would then marry with his own mother, Jocasta. Despite their attempt to thwart the oracle by leaving the child to be exposed, their plans go awry and the prophesy is fulfilled. When the plague is on the land, the oracle is again consulted. This time the utterance of the seer Tiresias is in the form of advice: "Expel the murderer of Laius!" The element of riddle is still present however, in that the askers do not yet know who the guilty party is, and in what is still the most outstanding instance of irony in the history of drama, Oedipus…not knowing that he himself is the guilty one…vows to obey the oracle implicitly.

Aristotle thought Oedipus Rex the most exemplary drama ever devised, and he may **still** be right. One of the reasons for its power and popularity not adduced by that philosopher, and perhaps better seen from our own distance, is the absolute and unquestioning acceptance by the audience of the axiology (the values, moral and ethical as well as religious) involved in its inner workings…and that in its turn makes a litmus of the play, a key to the character of the audience, to the nature of the Greeks and their religious beliefs. It's not a 'writerly' trick of Sophocles' that everything in his play turns on Orphic and oracular belief. That is part and parcel of the very nature of his dramatic enterprise that this aspect of existence is so fully manifested.

It is still the task of interpretation to enlighten us about the deeper feelings of religious emotion experienced by this people so close and necessary to us yet so distant as we look through telescopes of our own imperfect devising back across the great span of twenty centuries or so during which all traces of paganism were confidently suppressed if not blotted out entirely by the fathers of not only Catholicism but Protestantism and Judaism, and Islam as well. The established and entrenched felt no tolerance for Greek and Latin Paganism. Curiously, the history of Greek religion is itself a tale of accommodation of local and often bizarre religions to the general cultural gestalt. In this it was unlike those that followed and denied it, who felt no such spirit of tolerance and pragmatism. Cults, in ancient Greece, rose and fell rather on their own merit, need and popularity. There was no established priestly class to codify the general religion, or for that matter to suppress unorthodoxy. There were only Homer, Hesiod and Pindar…poets…to guide religious thought. The gods of their poems were as prone to jealousy, self-interest, lust and general chicanery as the humans. But the Greek gods laid no claim to moral perfection, as ours do. Still honor, courage and loyalty were defined by example. The Greeks had no *Bible*, no holy text to guide them chapter and verse, no *Pentateuch* to argue over, no 10 commandments, no manna on the desert to convince them they were God's only chosen ones.

Sophocles in the fifth century is more sophisticated than 8th century Homer in his delineation of religious matters affecting both the individual and the *polis*, yet they share certain beliefs, such as faith in oracles…Tiresias in *Oedipus Rex* and Cassandra in *Iliad*. Neither are listened to, with disastrous results, in both stories.

There is a fascination, quite apart from any cosmogony, with oracles and oracular utterances, and this entrancement may go all the way back to the time the first loudmouth hazarded a guess which came to pass exactly as he or she said it would. Second sight it is called, a kind of sense beyond the five or six we ordinarily experience, and when the endowment is obvious and the trick is repeated over and over the sibyl, seer or bakkid gains credibility and status as well, and in Greece it might become in effect an office, in the form of a shrine; it is assumed that the human involved is but a vessel and a voice for the expression of the god's will, advice or prediction. At Delphi the Pythoness spoke in a trance.

Melampus the Argonaut, healer and diviner, who must have been what we would call 'the ship's doctor' on Jason's Argosy, learned his secrets of healing by virtue of befriending and saving a family of reptiles. As he slept after the rescue the snakes licked his ears and it was in this way that he learned his miraculous cures. We may see the relationship between the serpent as symbol and medicine still in the caduceus.

Melampus was also able to listen to the animals. Having been imprisoned by his enemies, and again while napping, he overheard the termites in the wooden roof above his head, and found out from their conversation that their job of chewing through the rafters would be finished the next day. When he woke Melampus called to his jailer and begged to be put in another cell as the roof of his was about to collapse. They may have laughed, but they moved him, and when the ceiling fell the following day, his captors freed Melampus and befriended him, recognizing his powers.

The unfortunate Orestes who murdered his mother as was predicted in an oracle, later used the prophecy in his own defense, claiming that his parricide was, in effect, 'written.' This was considered a mitigating circumstance.

ORACLES IN HISTORY

As Plutarch relates in his *Lives*, the famous general Pyrrhus heard from an oracle that he would meet his doom when he saw a wolf fighting with a bull. Having stormed the town of Argos, Pyrrhus was trapped in the town square, in hand-to-hand combat with the residents. In the midst of this desperate fighting Pyrrhus saw a statue in the square of a wolf grappling with a bull. Pyrrhus recalled the oracle and he knew he was doomed. He was skulled by a tile thrown down from a rooftop by one of the town women just as Pyrrhus was about to slay her son.

It is difficult when looking at ancient Greece to separate mythology, legend and history, the past...fabulous as it may have been...was so inextricably linked in their thinking with the present they were living.

In *Anabasis*, variously translated as *The March Upcountry* , or *The Persian Expedition*, Xenophon gives an account of the daily life of the common Greek warrior that provides pregnant clues to the everyday thinking and beliefs of the ordinary Greek of the time. Writing his book presumably from diaries and journals he made on the expedition, which occurred just beyond the peak of the 'Classical Age' of Pericles, Plato, et. al. just at the end of the Peloponnesian Wars. Xenophon, an Athenian, a one-time student of Socrates, was invited by Cyrus to join an expedition into Persia, along with a mercenary army of 10,000 Greeks, mostly Spartans. The expedition failed of its purpose. In the battle Cyrus was killed, his army surrendered, and his Greek mercenaries, though themselves undefeated, having in fact advanced their own front five miles—apparently literally through a wall of human flesh—now found themselves surrounded by a million or so Persians, **all** of them now on the other side.

Invited to a parley with the Persians under a flag of truce the Greek generals were treacherously murdered, but Greeks being Greeks they just bumped everyone up a grade (sergeants to captains, etc.), and Xenophon, who had gone on the expedition merely as chronicler, found himself elected general, since it was his plan for their escape that was adopted...its acceptance assured because, just as Xenophon finished proposing his plan to the assembled soldiers, one among them sneezed, at which the others shouted 'elelu,' a sneeze in the desert being so uncommon that none of them doubted it was a sign of approval from Zeus.

In his famous book Xenophon recorded his small army's 1,500 mile trek to the sea, through enemy territory, over mountains, through snow, fighting rear-guard, the canny Athenian leading his tough Spartans, Achaians, Athenians, Arcadians, et.al., and the tale is as down-to-Earth and true-to-life as any modern war correspondent's wires home. The soldiers slept in the snow, letting it cover them for the warmth it retained, just as the G.I.'s did at Bastogne in 1945 AD, and they got frostbite, they foraged and shared and bargained with the natives, and stole (not outside the ethic of a Spartan warrior), and did what they were ordered to do...still a Greek army was more democratic than any modern army, and could strike or sit down, and had to be convinced before they moved...and yet when they fought, their strength lay in cohesion and iron discipline. However they might argue before the battle, once decided they 'sang the paean' as they charged, which must have sounded like a death hymn to the ears of the Persians.

It was a hymn to Paean, a god of sorts, an aspect of Apollo, who appears in *Iliad*, and this provides a clue to the success of Greek armies against their non-Greek neighbors. Not simply their piety came to their aid; they 'had an attitude.' It is one found commonly in Kipling. There seems not a nickel's worth of difference between a sergeant in any Greek army and one sent out by Her Majesty the Queen a couple of millennia later to keep the peace in India. It was an arrogant attitude. The average Greek looked upon those who could not speak Greek as *barbaroi*, as people who go 'ba ba!' That's what it sounded like to a Greek soldier.

The Greek warrior felt he had an edge, that he was as good as ten of the enemy. This self-image relates to success, and to the wedding of tradition and technology. In that ancient time tradition was more important than technology. Whether the Greeks had better weapons than the Persians may be a matter of doubt; they certainly had better tactics and discipline, and every soldier in that small army felt himself a part of a tradition that went back to Homer. The stories, the poetry, the deeds of gods and men were known to these soldiers and they felt the heroic spirit. Homer had taught them lessons of heroism and honor, of resourcefulness too, and the notion that courage is one of the few things over which the individual spirit has control, and one has a feeling reading Xenophon that the common foot soldier saw himself in all instances, and no matter where he went, in company with his gods. But not forgetting the practical realities of survival, and not depending slavishly upon his gods to do everything, he could fight with fearless courage, persistence and determination, knowing that the mob armies of the Great King would pull him and his comrades literally and individually to pieces, that failure and defeat meant death, torture, mutilation, crucifixion, decapitation...or worse.

There were no guides to their escape, so they prayed to Zeus Savior as well as Apollo, and sacrificed and read the entrails at every juncture of decision. At one point on the journey, Xenophon was all out of animals to sacrifice, except for the ox that pulled his cart. "Blow the cart," he said (or words to that effect), and sacrificed the ox. This time he got favorable reports so perhaps his sacrifice truly pleased the god, particularly since the beast was not just one out of the herd...but the **last** one! As a parable that's almost Christian. Xenophon, however, says it happened that way and I believe him, and when he says that he brought home through battle after battle, against overwhelming odds, through hostile country and mountains, through snow and cold, 8,600 of his 10,000 warriors, I believe that too, since he brought the evidence with him. And indeed Xenophon's entire account is a testament to the reverence the Greek had for individual human worth.

As they were their own worst and most terrible antagonists in their internecine struggles, the Greeks were also their own harshest critics. Xenophon wouldn't think of lying in his narrative, just as Homer did not intend to tell lies, even about the gods. Everything in *Iliad* is believed by its author (or authors). Heinrich Schliemann understood that and discovered the site of Troy, simply following Homer's descriptions of the site, the city's distance from the sea, the marshy terrain, the Scamander river, the heights...while the archaeologists who missed it, did so because they dismissed *Iliad* as a fanciful tale full of unlikely gods and heroes. But Homer was at the beginning of something, and even if his poem covered events taking place 300 years earlier, mysteriously almost, there was no loss of energy.

It is not surprising, not in every way, that the personage we know as 'Homer' was more likely a string of poets handling the material, though it says much of the faith in what is contained in the text and is perfectly coherent as a description of a culture and a set of beliefs about honor, courage, cleverness and governance as intentional as if it were, like Moses commandments, a blueprint for a society to follow, and indeed, in more ways than expected, that was exactly what happened. 400 years after the poetry and 800 or so after the event, the average soldier in Xenophon's little army could still see himself as participating in the same world, with the same gods, as those depicted in that ancient account. He took it all to be part of his own history, gods, heroes, oracles, omens, belief in the truth of augury, divination...indeed these were considered sciences, as complex in discipline as they were arcane.

But a curious thing. Xenophon acted as his own priest, which is to say that as a 'gentleman,' author and general, he also knew how to read the entrails of the sacrifice. Like the Jews of a later age, the Greeks had no priestly class. In the latter case, one never quite developed, perhaps because of the evolutionary, inclusive, agglomerate nature of Greek religion. No single 'doctrine' ever prevailed, no set of beliefs ever became institutionalized and dogmatic. Greek religion fell short of the unity necessary to develop a canon, and a priesthood to provide authority and demand obedience was never seen as called for. Yet an individual may act as his own priest, may cultivate his own relationship with Heaven, and knows the rules of behavior and of ceremony as a matter of course.

> I have enough religion for my own purposes.
> —Socrates

Alexander followed Xenophon into Asia, and like the Athenian, did not neglect the ceremonies. No sooner did Alexander set foot on the Asian continent than he made a sacrifice to the ghost of Priam, to placate that very distant King of Ilium. Alexander also crowned with wreaths the tomb of Achilles, from whom he claimed descent. Again, it must be remembered that those Homeric heroes who preceded Alexander did so by eight centuries. Yet the young Macedonian king felt both a kinship and a responsibility to their spirits. And in effect, he did exactly the right thing at the right moment, deifying himself as he invaded Asia. It was the right sort of psychology, for the Medes and the rest would much more readily allow themselves to be conquered by a god than a mortal. The mother of Alexander's ancestor Achilles was Thetis, a sea-goddess.

At Gordian, soon after this, Alexander cut the famous knot. An oracle had foretold that whoever could undo the intricate knot of Gordius would conquer Asia. Having tried in vain to untie it, Alexander drew his sword and hacked it through. But he was nonetheless obeying the prophecy, actually adding that fillip of added truth so often found in oracles. Of course the task would be accomplished with the sword! Interesting to add perhaps that all who had tried before Alexander...and failed...none thought simply to cut the knot...however impulsive Alexander's act might seem. And the prophesy was fulfilled.

THE ORACLE AT DELPHI

Apollo pursued Python who fled to the Oracle of Mother Earth at Delphi. The
Snake God was mate to Delphyne, the oracular aspect of Hera, or her mother,
Gea, the original Earth Mother. Python had tried to violate Apollo's mother Leto
and was surprised by the god. Wounded by Apollo's arrows, Python returned to
his own mother/mate for safety. Apollo pursued him. Python was slain; then
Apollo usurped the shrine, and extracted from the god Pan its oracular secrets.

If there seems to be an incestuous aspect about this, that's common among
the Olympians. The sin of Oedipus in Sophocles' great play of that name is
hubris, or pride, in that he imitates, however unwittingly, the gods in lying with
his own mother. The ancient Greeks were as parabolic about human concerns as
anyone else in that time, and seeking to explain the incunabula of existence, seeking to explain the psychological conundrums life itself presents, invented poetry,
then drama. It was a very imaginative process of sorting out what's necessary and
what's feasible. In any event, the tellers of these stories, poets and playwrights,
struck chords deep in the psyche of their hearers. What is natural and perhaps
necessary for the gods must be denied to mortals. As Jocasta warns Oedipus:
'These things are such as only happen in the dreams of men.' Future shades of
Freud! Not for everyone…in fact, only the province of the gods…and the sub-
conscious…whose ways are mysterious and terrible to mortals.

The goddess Hera is the twin sister of Zeus, as well as his wife, and Hera, as
Earth Mother, is consort to her son Python. Python also pursues Leto, Apollo's
mother, and Apollo, who is jealous of his mother's pursuer must 'scotch the
snake' that creeps into her boudoir. One may be reminded of Hamlet (mistak-
enly) killing Polonius hidden behind the arras in Gertrude's bedroom, taking the
old man for Claudius, the usurper of Hamlet's place. Hamlet also pursues
Claudius to his death, but dies himself (hubris again?). Themes like this are the
'guts' of drama, as the Greeks well knew as they watched the doings of gods and
men and the inevitable consequences of ideas translated into deeds enacted in the
theater, or in the declamations of poets.

The Greeks leapt into the mysterious and the forbidden with what Homer
might call 'the courage of a fly,'…or with the fearless and playful curiosity of
whelps toying with scorpions. They took everything as instructive…dreams,

poetry, portents. They wanted to know if the ways of the gods could be known, or if the future could be read as easily as the past.

Explanations give credence. Why Delphi? Whence come these oracular powers? Can they be relied upon? According to the story Apollo, triumphant over the snake god, vests his oracular authority with the Delphic priestess...the Pythoness...who speaks 'in tongues,' for the Gods speak their own language. Her unintelligible and perhaps frenzied utterances are decoded by her attendant priests into hexametric poetry, the meaning of which, though the answer may emerge as a riddle, should be clear at least to the one who asked the question.

A more mundane version of the founding of the Delphic shrine tells the story of Coretas, a shepherd tending his flocks on the side of Parnassus, who came upon a fissure from whence emanated a gas. Sniffing at it, Coretas began to prophesy, spoke in strange languages and while in his trance was overheard by others. When he recovered his normal sense he remembered nothing of the event. The shrine it is said, was built over this fissure. The priestess descended into the chamber built over the fissure when she was preparing to answer questions. Why a priestess? Why not Coretas, or someone like him? I think the answer is in the relationship of the female with the Earth. It is the temple of Earth after all, the navel of the world, and dedicated to Gea.

Its origins according to Plutarch go back 3,000 years from his time. That would put it into the third millennium, long before the habit of writing took hold, so any view of the origins of the Shrine must indeed be murky. The place was supposed by the Greeks to be the navel or center of the Earth, which is to say the center of the Greek universe. There was a sacred stone, almost conical, which was called the '**omphalos**,' or navel. It was found there quite early and undoubtedly was sacred to prehistoric people of the region, all the way back (beyond Stonehenge, beyond Altamira, etc.) Being of ancient lineage, whether a rock or a family, carried a certain aura of having been there when the gods were there! It was natural for the Greeks to see religious connections, to be sensitive to things...and in a serious way...that to us seem commonplace. The Delphic oracle was consulted mainly on religious matters, but the religious connection extended to many other things and events.

The most ancient oracle of Greece was that of Zeus at Dodona-and it was this oracle, according to Herodotus, who named the gods, 'with their honors, attributes, etc.' This most remote and ancient shrine...far Dodona' the Greeks would say, perhaps with the same intimation as we would say 'way up North,' implying that it was a piece to travel, and this may have had some influence on its credibility as both a shrine and an oracle, at least at first; but as the cultural value of oracular shrines increased and expanded they became more and more media in the general sense, and functioned as places of meeting between people from all parts, exchanging ideas, gossip, news, views and information. This may account in part for the increasing popularity of Delphi...it was much more centrally located, it grew and surpassed all others in popularity and credibility, located as it was on the slope of Parnassus...a most holy mountain...hard by the Gulf of Corinth, and not so far from Corinth, Athens, Thebes and Sparta.

At the beginning of the 6th century B. C. the town of Crisa lay in the valley below Delphi at the entrance to the path up the mountain leading to the shrine, and more and more Crisa exploited its position, selling trinkets and charging admission...this despite the religious displeasure, the admonitions, and finally the warnings of the other Greeks who visited; and in one of the few instances of Greek solidarity, the other states, citing the importance as well as the sacred nature of the shrine, in a holy war, attacked Crisa, slew all its inhabitants, razed the town and forbade any future rebuilding. Thus the virtue and holiness of the shrine was seen important enough to be protected against control and corruption by any one city or group at the expense of the shrine or the culture in general.

The shrine kept the states in touch with each other, affirmed pan-Hellenic Greek culture. Games were instituted at Delphi as well, in the even year between the Olympian games at Elis. These included of course dramatic presentations, poetry readings and musical contests. The spirit was no less important to them than the physique, and the mind with its personal aesthetic and spiritual sensibilities should also be cultivated, exercised and displayed. The Graces always attendant on the Dionysian were Brilliance, Bloom and Joy. These were important to the Greeks (the Spartans perhaps excepted: the contradiction that proves the rule, as was their wont, the Spartans could see no use in joy as they saw no use in philosophy.) In general however the Greeks, and the ancients, had a quite different hold on the spiritual than we moderns...even the Spartans, who could be wonderfully pragmatic, could still and at the same moment be deeply and sincerely religious, and saw no contradiction in this. Now, in the modern world, with the triumph of science over 'superstition' we are obsessed by the material, the practical, and it seems to us illogical, even dangerous, to be spiritual in a material world.

The oracle initiated no policy. The Pythoness merely 'counseled' and that only conditionally, and in riddles. Thus the oracle did not find itself at odds with any state, and never interfered on behalf of any 'side,' save its own.

Sometimes it was good news, reassuring to the askers. Before the battle of Marathon one bacis prophesied:

> **Yes. by Thermodon's stream and the bed of grass by Asopus, there shall be conflict between the Greeks and the screaming barbarians; there indeed many shall fall beyond what need be and must be of the Medes who carry the bow,when Fate's day has overtaken them.**

One oracle or another was consulted (with appropriate offerings and ceremonies) before one took any journey, embarked on any enterprise...no new colony would be founded, no general would hazard a battle, no admiral leave shore without some consultation and reply; and upon success, say in victory over an enemy, a tithe (tenth) of the spoil would go to adorn the temple of the oracle, sometimes even the 'first fruits' of success. Needless to say, a shrine, such as the one at Delphi...the most sought after...would become wealthy beyond imagining. It is a testimonial to the universal belief in these auguries that even the Persians, when they invaded Greece, consulted the Delphic oracle, and received the reply that the Persians would fail soon after the sack of Delphi. The temple was not robbed, but the Persians were defeated anyway. The Greeks thought nothing of this defensive prevarication, since the oracle had a right to defend herself, and the Persians were foreigners bent on mischief anyway.

Perhaps the most famous of oracular utterances was that given to the Athenians in the same war against the Persians:

> **Wretched ones, why sit you here? Flee and begone to remotest**
> **Ends of Earth, leaving your homes, high places in circular city;**
> **For neither the head abides sound, no more than the feet or the body;**
> **Fire pulls all down, and sharp Ares, driving his Syrian-bred horses.**
> **Many a fortress besides, and not yours alone shall he ruin.**

Many the temples of God to devouring flames he shall give
them.
There they stand now, the sweat of terror streaming down
from them.
They shake with fear; from the rooftops black blood in del-
uging torrents.
They have seen the forthcoming destruction, and evil
sheerly constraining.
Get you gone out of the shrine! Blanket your soul with
your sorrows.

One can well imagine the chagrin…the cold fear perhaps…of the Athenian
envoys, for there was little doubt about the meaning of the words of the
Pythoness. Ares, the god of war, will make good use of Syrian-bred horses, the
temples on the Acropolis shall burn, and the town about the hill below shall be
destroyed. Notwithstanding the harsh words of the oracle the Athenians sent
again to Delphi, this time going as suppliants, looking for more hopeful auspices,
and the second time received the following reply:

No: Athena cannot appease great Zeus of Olympus
With many eloquent words and all her cunning counsel
To you I declare again this word, and make it as iron:
All shall be taken by foemen, whatever within his border
Cecrops contains, and whatever the glades of sacred
Cithaeron—
Yet to Tritogeneia shall Zeus, loud-voiced, give a present,
A wall of wood, which alone shall abide unsacked;
Well shall it serve yourselves and your children in days to come.
Do not abide the charge of horse and foot that come on you,
A mighty host from the landward side, but withdraw
before it.
Turn your back in retreat; on another day you shall face
them.
Salamis, isle divine, you shall slay many children of
women,
Either when seed is sown or again when the harvest is
gathered.

This second reply did hold out some hope in its assurance that the 'gift of Zeus,' a wooden wall, would not be sacked; but the old wooden wall about the city had long since been torn down. The clever **strategos** Themistocles interpreted the message, saying that by 'wooden walls' the Pythoness meant the Athenian navy, the 'wooden walls' being the wooden ships which would prove decisive in the defense of their homeland against the Persians.

The oracle was an instruction to move the entire Attic populace to the island of Salamis as well as an assurance of what would follow. The victory of the Greeks at the Battle of Salamis over a much larger Persian navy confirmed the truth of Themistocles' interpretation...and the oracle's powers, and indeed explained at last the final two lines of the cryptic utterance. Another oracle gave further assurance of ultimate victory over the Persians:

> **Mad is their hope, having sacked the glory of Athens;**
> **Then shall bright Justice quench their savage wrath, child of Hybris,**
> **For all its fury so dreadful, thinking to drink off destruction;**
> **For bronze shall encounter bronze,**
> **With blood the sea shall be crimsoned by Ares,**
> **And Greece's free day shall the wide-heard voice of Cronides**
> **Bring to fulfillment...yes...holy Victory shall bring it to pass.**

Cronides is Zeus, Son of Cronos, in his temporal aspect. The oracle urges patience. 'Hybris' is overweening pride, here styled a child of wrath. Pride goeth before the fall, as the proverb has it.

It is not our intention to explain away, or for that matter, to advocate the truth of, the utterances of ancient oracles. Yet we must acknowledge, concerning the beliefs of others of any era, that their world was as real to them as our modern world of science is to us. If we can believe Herodotus and other ancient historians, the Delphic oracle had an uncanny rate of success, and had a knowledge of distant events which could not have been available even with the most efficient network of spies.

According to Herodotus the great King Croesus faithfully followed the oracle's advice after an incident in which the king sent to all the oracles around and received their replies. Reading them Croesus was dissatisfied with all but one...that from the Delphic Pythoness who complained in hexameters:

> Number of sand grains I know, and also the measures of
> Ocean;
> I understand him that is dumb and can hearken to the
> voiceless.
> A smell steals over my senses, the smell of a hard-shelled
> tortoise,
> Seethed in bronze with the meat of lambs, mingled
> together;
> Bronze is the base beneath, and bronze the vestment upon
> it.

Croesus had sent his messengers to the various oracles with the instruction that they should arrive and ask their question of the oracle precisely on the hundredth day after their departure from Croesus...not before, not after...exactly one hundred days. Telling no one Croesus on the hundredth day chopped up some lamb and turtle...an unlikely combination...and cooked it in a bronze kettle...and the oracle had sniffed it out! Therefore, to Croesus, only the Delphic oracle was truly an oracle.

Sometimes the Pythoness needed some help, as in the case of Leonidas, the Spartan king, hero of Thermopylae, who heard from the oracle that Greece would be spared but a king must die, one descended from Heracles.

> For all of you who dwell
> In Sparta of the broad avenues
> Your city is great and glorious,
> But by the manhood of Persia
> She shall be sacked...or she shall not,
> But then Lacaedaemon's Watcher
> Shall mourn for a king that shall die,
> From Heracles' race descended...

Since he was of that lineage Leonidas took the reply as naming him, and so willingly and intentionally sacrificed himself at Thermopylae. The oracle was often thus taken as a virtual instruction.

Much depended upon interpretation. A misinterpreted prophecy could mean disaster, as in the case of the Spartan Cleomenes who, while besieging Argos sent a question and received a reply from the oracle that he would conquer Argos. But Cleomenes found that the prophesy had been fulfilled when he burned down a grove near the city which he learned afterward was called The Grove of Argus. Knowing the playfulness of the Pythia he took his army back to Sparta, and was excused his failure to pursue the siege when he explained the reason for his action. The Spartans were as religious[6] as they were warlike.

The mad King Cambyses confused the two cities of Ecbatana (one in Media, the other in Syria) named in an oracular reply and attacked the wrong town, where instead of the promised victory he found death.

Another religious war was fought around the Delphic shrine in 356 BC. The temple was taken and held by a Phocian general named Philomelus. He was concerned that the Pythoness should continue to give out prophesies, and was eager himself to get some 'good news' from her. But the Pythoness was stubborn and refused to sit on her tripod. To her these Phocians, Greek though they may be, were still intruders. The frustrated general tried to force her to sit in the holy place, but when he laid hands on her she told him in plain language to do as he would. This Philomelus took to be the oracle he sought, the sanction for what he planned. In this case, the interpretation was far amiss. Philomelus at first borrowed then robbed the treasury of the shrine (still taking the forced 'oracle' as assent and approval). He used the plate, the silver, the golden basins and tripods like booty, hiring vast levies of mercenaries, since none of the legitimate states would help him in his war. It is anticlimactic almost to add the final scene of the final battle in which Philomelus, trapped, surrounded by his victorious enemies at the edge of the cliff, chooses to leap to his death. True to historical fact, this story must have been told again and again as a moral of impiety, sacrilege and the price of profanation.

The great and lucky general Timoleon, prior to his campaigns in Sicily, had only to enter the shrine at Delphi to be given his oracle. The wall inside the shrine was decorated with wreaths embroidered with images of victory and golden crowns. One of these 'unaccountably' fell from the wall and struck Timoleon. Needless to say his Sicilian wars were phenomenally successful.

The Lydian tyrant Alyattes inherited a war from his father, Sadyattes, against the Milesians. In the 11th year of the war, the young prince Alyattes took over and burnt the corn crop of his enemies. But he failed to take the wind into account and the fire destroyed the local temple of Athena. Not long after this Alyattes fell sick and stayed ill for some time. At last he sent to Delphi to con-

---

[6]Tut, tut. 'Superstition' is a term we use to describe the other guy's religion.

sult the Pythia. The suppliants were told that no oracle would be granted to Aly-attes till the temple to Athena destroyed in the fire was rebuilt. The difficulty for Alyattes was that the enemy was now between him and the temple. This forced him to an armistice and a reconciliation, in honor of which he erected not one but two temples to Athena. Shortly thereafter, it is said, he recovered his health.

As we said, no Greek colony would be sent out without first consulting the oracle. The Greeks, in that relatively barren country, or in the confines of an island kept the population of their cities small, within manageable limits. When the number of people grew too large for comfort in the polis it was time to found a colony. These colonies were not under the control of the mother country as happened in later history, but were independent, and the ties of clan and blood were thought sufficient for favor in future trade, or for protection of the new-born city-state, as with Syracuse and its parent, Corinth. Timoleon was a Corinthian for instance who went to the aid of Syracuse at their request.

Sometimes the Pythoness would take a hand in the decision to send out a colony, as in the case of Thera, whose king, consulting the oracle on other mat-ters, was told by the priestess to found a colony in Libya. The Thereans had no idea where in the world Libya was, and ignored the instruction. Thereafter no rain fell on Thera for seven years. The Thereans went back to Delphi and again were told 'Colonize Libya.' This time they found out where it was and sent a colony. These folks however founded their city on an island just off the coast of Libya. They ran onto hard times and were unable to make a go of it. So again they sent to the oracle and complained that they had followed the Pythia's instructions, but to no avail. The priestess answered:

So you know Libya, land of sheepfolds, better than I!
You haven't gone there! I have!
I wonder indeed at your knowledge.

They went back and tried again with a new colony on the mainland, and fared much better. The story illustrates the wonderful resonance in the Greek mind of oracular faith and the wisdom ascribed to it. We've repeated the account in brief to illustrate the oracle's influence, and its role as counselor, rather like the *I Ching* of the Chinese, which has an uncanny knack of homing in on the unre-solved and unspoken.

And then at times the Pythoness seemed vexed at people's lack of common sense, as when the Megareans came to be advised where to build their new colony. She advised them to build their new city "across from the city of the blind men." She meant the site of what was to become known as Byzantium, then Constantinople, now Istanbul. Situated on the European shore at the entrance from the Euxine (Black Sea) to the Propontis, thence to the Aegean. Its position allowed it to dominate the area, and was itself easily defended. Chalcedon, on the Asian shore, had apparently been built by blind men, since its position is so obviously the inferior choice. The joke may have been long current. The Megareans in any case knew just where to go. The town, as a great city, bested all of them and lasted longer, was the seat of a thousand-year empire, the see of a great religion, and so on. Small wonder the Pythoness has the reputation for sage advice.

It may be argued that the Spartans were the most religious of the Greeks, and this is evidenced in part by the fact that they kept an office of Pythian, two to each of their two kings. These Pythians were permanently assigned to consult with the oracle. The priestess was consulted by Sparta so often that the shrine was jokingly referred to as Sparta's "Foreign Office."

In this connection there is the story of Sparta's unique double kingship that illustrates perhaps the Pythia's sense of humor. Aristodemus, who as the story goes, was king when the Spartans conquered the land they afterward called their own, had twin sons and died soon after their birth. The Spartans wished to make the elder of the two king, but their mother would not reveal which was born first. The Spartans sent to Delphi to enquire of the god what they should do. The priestess told them to make both of the children kings but to honor more the elder.

Finally the Spartans worked it out for themselves, watching the mother and observing which of the children she seemed to favor, which she bathed first, for instance, and thereby determined which to honor. Of course they also did as they were instructed, and thereby began the double kingship of Sparta. The story explains of course not only the reason for having two kings, but how to tip the balance when differences arise. Seniority.

As in the case of the Thereans, the oracle sometimes had bigger things in mind for those who came to seek its advice. Tisamenus the Elean consulted the oracle because he wanted to ask a question about his children, but the oracle told him a strange thing: That he would win the '5 Great Contests.' He took this to mean olympic contests and went into training and in fact came within a fall of taking the laurel in wrestling. Tisamenus styled himself a prophet and followed the Spartan army in its adventures. He was obviously, like many Greeks, an admirer of the Spartiates, and it was they who suggested to Tisamenus that the Pythoness meant something quite different when she used the phrase '5 great contests,' and they invited Tisamenes to share the leadership of their army, at that moment preparing to fight the Persian host at Platea. Whatever intuition prompted the Spartans (perhaps an oracle unknown to us was given to them) they were willing to pay the price Tisamenus asked...Spartan citizenship for him and his brother. This was the only time in history that that honor was bestowed. The Greeks defeated the Persians at Platea, and Tisamenus, whose prophetic powers apparently improved, by them helped the Spartans to win the four campaigns that followed the defeat of Mardonius.

Neoptolemus, the son of Achilles, who more than equaled his father in irascible arrogance, went to the Pythoness at Delphi to demand satisfaction for the death of his father. Neoptolemus believed Apollo to be responsible for the arrow that pierced the heel of Achilles and caused his death.

The Pythoness showed him the door. Enraged by her curt dismissal, Neoptolemus and his Myrmidons attacked, plundered and burnt the shrine. Still, in an example of perhaps the most unmitigated gall in history, Neoptolemus returned to the shrine, still in ruins but being rebuilt, to ask of the Pythoness why his wife remained barren.

He was told by the Pythoness to sacrifice, which he did, but when he saw the haunches of his fat oxen going to feed (as was the custom) the retainers of the shrine, again Neoptolemus became furious and tried by force to prevent it.

"Let us be rid of this troublesome son of Achilles," the Pythoness said, at which one of the priests dispatched Neoptolemus with a sacrificial knife.

"Bury him beneath our new threshold," the Pythoness ordered. "He was a warrior, and provided he has repented of his insult to Apollo, he will guard our sanctuary against attack."

THE ORACLE OF MOPSUS

It was Mopsus who shamed the prophet Calchas, seer-in-residence to Agamemnon and the Greeks who assailed and conquered Troy. It had been foretold by the Delphic oracle that Calchas would die after meeting a prophet better than himself. On his return from Troy Calchas met Mopsus, the son of Manto, who was the daughter of Tiresias, and his father was Apollo.

Calchas, on their meeting, challenged Mopsus to compute the number of figs that would be harvested from a fig tree standing nearby.

"Ten thousand figs," Mopsus answered without hesitation, "plus an Aeginetan bushel, carefully weighed…and a single fig left over."

Calchas laughed at the temerity of Mopsus, but when the tree was picked clean, Mopsus' figure proved accurate. Then, taking his shot, Mopsus inquired of Calchas: "That sow over there, about to litter…how many piglets will she deliver?"

"Eight," Calchas guessed, "And she will farrow within nine days."

Mopsus closed his eyes. "I make it three piglets, one of them male, by midday tomorrow."

When, the next day Mopsus again proved correct, Calchas, it is said, died of a broken heart.

The ghost of Calchas later had a shrine on Mount Drium in Daunia, which was well-known as a dream oracle.

The oracle of Mopsus could be found at Claros; and another, with Amphilocus, at Mallus. This second site was apparently the scene of Mopsus' death, where he and Amphilocus in a dispute over which would rule the city of Mallus, fought a duel which resulted in the death of both. After their deaths their ghosts became staunch friends, and the shrine they shared was considered by many to be even more accurate than that of Delphi.

THE ORACLE OF AMPHIARAUS

Amphiaraus is perhaps an example of the determinism found often in Greek religion. He foresaw his own death in the war of the *Seven Against Thebes*, that all would die except Adrastus, himself included, in the ill-fated attempt to take the city. Yet he went. Was it bravery or a deep-rooted fatalism, or both, that prompted him? It was said the Earth swallowed him as he retreated from the battle. A shrine was erected to him at Oropus, and there oracles were given by means of dreams.

The Oracle of Asclepius

Another dream oracle was that of Asclepius in Epidaurus. The various oracles functioned as we have seen, in a variety of ways, usually appropriate to the situation. The power and dignity of Apollo's shrine at Delphi made it in effect everyone's 'foreign office;' that is, questions of great importance were taken there. Likewise Zeus's oracle at Dodona, because of its great age and reputation. Asclepius, being the apotheosis of the physician, his shrine customarily answered questions of health and well-being. The visitor there was instructed to lie down, perhaps given some sedative potion to drink, to sleep and to dream, and in that dream would come the answer to his question about his health.

The birth of Asclepius is both strange and significant. His mother, Coronis, was the daughter of Phlegyas, King of the Lapiths. His father was Apollo. When he was obliged to make a journey to Delphi, the god left a snow-white crow to watch Coronis, who was already pregnant with Apollo's child. While he was gone Coronis took Ischys, for whom she had long had a secret passion, to her bed. The crow flew off to tattle to Apollo, expecting to be rewarded. But the jealous god instead was angry that the crow had not plucked out the eyes of Ischys, and with a curse turned the crow's feathers from white to black.

Apollo complained of Coronis' infidelity to his sister Artemis, who shot a quiver of arrows at the unfaithful woman and killed her. Then Apollo felt remorse, but it was too late to keep the soul of Coronis from Tartarus. Her funeral pyre was already ablaze. Quickly Apollo had Hermes cut her open to deliver the still living child from her womb. This child Apollo named Asclepius, and sent him to the centaur Cheiron to learn the arts of medicine.

Asclepius was a mortal who attained to godhead by virtue of his skill and his contributions to medicine and thus to mankind. The most famous allusion to Asclepius was the remark by Socrates as he was about to drink the poison hemlock. "Remember," the philosopher said, "I owe a cock to Asclepius."

The joke is lost on modern readers. Asclepius, being the patron god of medicine and health, one was supposed to make sacrifice in gratitude upon getting well after illness. Socrates' joke then is that life is the illness from which he expects now to recover. An Orphic jest, again not too unlike one a Christian saint or martyr might make…not very different from "I go now to meet my father."

THE ORACLE AT TEGYRAE

The Delians, expelled from their country by the Athenians, sent to Delphi, look-ing for a way out of their predicament. The oracle told them to seek the place where Apollo was born and perform certain sacrifices there. Since they had always thought that Apollo was born in Delos they were puzzled, but the Pythoness added that a crow would show them the way. On their search, stop-ping at an inn, they overheard the proprietress talking to some strangers about the oracle at Tegyrae. On departing the strangers said goodbye to the proprietress by name: 'Corone'…which in their language means 'crow.' The Delians therefore dutifully performed their sacrifices at Tegyrae and soon (after the Spartan defeat of Athens) were returned to their homeland.

THE ORACLE OF TROPHONIUS

The story of the origin of the oracle of Trophonius is indeed strange. Trophonius and his brother Agamedes were said to be the architects of the temple at Delphi. They were after that contracted to build a treasury for King Hyrieus, whose wealth was reputed to be vast. In building the vault the brothers contrived to cre-ate a secret entrance through which a grown man could just fit, and they used this entrance to pilfer the king's treasure, bit by bit. But the king, who kept strict accounts, found that instead of growing richer as he thought, he was getting poorer; yet still he could not see how. Then one night while the brothers were pilfering Agamedes got stuck in the passageway. Realizing that he could not extricate his brother, and certain that Agamedes was bound to confess and impli-cate him under torture, Trophonius, with apologies, cut off his brother's head. This would also thwart identification. Grim as the story sounds, its retelling appealed to the Greek fondness for the clever. And finally, Trophonius himself was, with characteristic Greek irony, swallowed up by the Earth.

This story serves to explain at least why the cave of Trophonius was barely large enough for a person to slip through, and why the seekers were put into a depressed and claustrophobic state of mind, why they were said to be grim and downcast on their re-emergence. Although the cave is mentioned quite often in ancient texts, its whereabouts is today unknown.

The story told by Timarchus in Plutarch's dialogue 'Socrates Daimonion' is a fascinating bit of reportage. Timarchus was the boyhood friend of Socrates' son Lamprocles. Both youngsters died young, Lamprocles preceding Timarchus by only a few days. Timarchus had a foretelling of his own death, and requested of Socrates that he be buried alongside his friend. What he didn't tell Socrates, but reported to other friends, was an account of his descent into the Cave of Trophonius on his recent visit to Lebadea.

"I descended into the cave," he told them, "and was at first confronted only by total darkness. I prayed, and after a time, not knowing if I was awake or dreaming, I seemed to get a blow on the head and the sutures of my skull parted to release my soul; which rose joyfully into the ether, and I could see the stars and shining islands of light whirling in the firmament."

Timarchus went on to describe what to twentieth century ears sounds like a bona fide hallucination. After a description of the terrain, worthy of Edgar Allan Poe in its beauty of image and fullness of detail (but rather overlong for these confines) Timarchus looked down, he said, "and beheld a great chasm, like a sphere cut open, very deep and frightening, full of a welling turbulence, from which rose to my ears the most excruciating cries, howls and groans. I saw living, suffering creatures beyond number, wailing children, heard lamentations…men and women making a din of unintelligible but unmistakable anguish and woe."

Then a voice was heard by Timarchus, as the rest faded to background. Though he could not see the speaker he heard: "What would you know, Timarchus?"

"Everything," Timarchus replied. "For what is there that is not marvellous?"

There follow more descriptive passages, then the voice tells Timarchus that there are four principles that govern the universe: Life, Motion, Becoming and

Decay. He is told too that "every soul has some part in intellect, there being no soul without reason (intellect); still, the part of the soul that combines with the flesh and its passions is changed by pleasure and pain into an irrational state or condition." Then there is a description of souls in different states and stages, from the frenetic thrashings of those disturbed, to those in which the irrational element has been tamed, in which the true **daimonion** (the perfected spirit or soul) has taken charge, whose motions are even and well-directed.

"You will learn more of these things in two months time," the voice told him, then all faded and Timarchus was again lying near the entrance inside the cave where he awoke with a bad headache. Then having told his friends these things, Timarchus returned to Athens and prepared to die. After his death, when his friends finally related Timarchus' account to Socrates, the philosopher was quite put out that he'd never had a chance to question Timarchus himself about these matters.

THE ORACLE OF APIS

Many oracles seem too simple, too much like coney catchers, as in the accounts of the bull god Apis, whose oracle was at Memphis in Egypt. Visitors got answers to their questions via the bull's acceptance or refusal of offerings of food. If he ate, the answer would be favorable, if not, not. Which seems to mean that the bull must be asked a yes-or-no question. This is quite removed from the lofty hexametric riddles of the Pythia.

Many of the oracles were situated in caves, and one wonders again about subterranean emanations on that geologically unstable Greek peninsula. But again, the hallucination has its own reality. And there is the Orphic significance of a special wisdom coming from underground. With the Greeks we must consider the poetry of their belief.

In addition to the oracles we have mentioned, there were also the oracular shrines of Ammon, in Egypt, of Ptoion, in Boetia...even Tiresias has an oracle, and so did his daughter Manto! Perhaps there were as many shrines as there were cathedrals in France in a later age, a rich heritage of belief, without a doubt.

VI.

THE ROMANS

"...the Trojans are in Latium! Aeneas with his fleet and his vanquished gods proclaims himself King!"

—Virgil

THE SIBYL

The Sibyl of the Romans was not a goddess, however fabulous her life, her power and her fate. Wooed by Apollo, she asked him the boon of long life, years equal to the grains of sand she could hold in her two hands…but she neglected to ask that her youth be sustained over all those years, and falling from favor with Apollo she grew older, and older, and smaller and smaller…so old and so small that at last she disappeared and only her voice remained. In her relationship with Apollo she learned from him oracular secrets…as he had learned them from Pan at Delphi.

The Sibyl appeared, it is said, at the court of Tarquinius Superbus, the last king of Rome, (c. 525 BC) with a set of nine books of oracles in Greek, which she offered to him for a prohibitive price. Tarquin refused, whereupon the Sibyl burnt three of the books and offered the remaining six for the price of the original nine. Again the king declined. She burnt three more, then offered the last three again at the original price. Tarquin bought those that were left, and these books were consulted by the Romans in times of great catastrophes, drought or famine, not to discover the future but to find out why the gods were displeased and how to placate them. The texts of the oracles were destroyed by a fire in the capitol in 83 BC.

It was the Sibyl who guided Aeneas through the underworld in Virgil's epic poem, as that Trojan hero and legendary ancestor of Rome sought his dead father Anchises. Recall that Dante, centuries later would acknowledge his imitation by having Virgil guide him on a similar journey through the underworld. Of course Virgil had his model (the descent of Odysseus into the Underworld, where the hero meets his mother) in the author of *Odyssey*, Homer; the point here being that these notions and beliefs about a spiritual afterlife themselves enjoyed a healthy existence for many centuries, and bridged the pagan and Christian eras.

The Romans did not consult oracles as a matter of official policy, indeed, Augustus had 2,000 books of prophesies confiscated and consigned to the flames. Long before that the senate had confiscated several collections of oracular writings which no doubt met the same fate. The Sibyl's cave at Cumae (which was originally a Greek colony) was tolerated as virtually the only oracle on the peninsula. The temple of Fortuna at Praeneste might qualify, for oracles were given there, but mostly these were for popular use in answer to trivial questions and personal problems.

The silence then of oracles could be explained by their becoming simply obsolescent with the decline of one culture and the rise of another. Belief in and consultation of oracles was more a Greek habit than a Roman one.

Scholar and novelist Robert Graves made good use of the Sibyl in *I, Claudius*. In Graves' version of backstairs Rome in the Augustan Age, the Sibyl appears to Claudius, the lame, inveterate scholar and history buff, to tell him that his autobiographical manuscript detailing the lives and crimes of his own family…Tiberius, Livia, Caligula, Nero, et al…will be lost to posterity, only to be rediscovered after 2,000 years…and it is, by Robert Graves! The credibility so deftly accommodated, as playful as any oracle, lends charm to Professor Graves' wonderful historical narrative, actually based on Seutonius' *Lives of the Twelve Caesars*. And perhaps it hints at a persistence of awareness about oracles, and like many another 'fictional' narrative in the modern world, takes an audience still knowledgeable about such things as a given.

In the *Satyricon* of Petronius Arbiter, Nero's poet laureate, one of the characters claims that he has seen the Sibyl at Cumae, so small by that time that she was kept in a jar, suspended from a tripod, and when one of the children asked the Sibyl what she wished for, she said she wished for death.

From the Battle for Troy (c.1180 B.C.) to Desert Storm (1991 A.D.) oracles have had their say…and when listened to, have had a profound influence upon the most crucial historical events. Despite the centuries-long proscription of all superstition, fortune telling and heterodox prophetic belief by Christianity, and their general debunking by modern pragmatic science, things still happen which seem to have been long since foreseen.

Merlin was the fabulous wizard, magician and prophet who served as advisor to the legendary King Arthur. Myths abound and tales of Merlin's arcane knowledge and occult powers are multitudinous, though appearing as he does…if he did at all…in the shadowy area between legend and history there can be little known for certain about him. One English historian, Geoffrey of Monmouth, writing in the twelfth century treated Merlin as an actual historical personage. According to one more recent and fanciful author, Merlin's powers of prediction were the result of the fact that he lived backwards to Arthur's time from the Twentieth Century. Whether or not Merlin ever existed, his presence in

Arthurian legend illustrates the persistence in our cultural history of seers, wizards and prophets as having the ear of the great and thereby influencing events.

Christianity and the Dark Ages had a deleterious effect on the individual human psyche; and in the all-consuming, self-sacrificing love of some distant deity, civilized Europeans lost the sense of magic as it was understood in the spirit; then in the neglect of the self came also the loss of self-esteem. The belief in one's own spiritual power waned in proportion to giving up the self (and any responsibility in the matter) to God and His Paternal Ministers, entering into a suicidal sacrifice of the soul, I must say. And we seem to being doing it all over again in our relationship to the state, in the name of patriotism, seduced by that over-rated emotion, bowing to a flag or an institution, or some other witless modern invention that has nothing sacred fine or enduring about it.

By the time the universal spell of religion was broken by science, expediency and practical results it was too late to return to the old explanations, and that might be all for the best, except for the sense of loss, not just of magic, but of communion and responsibility. It's hard now to imagine a world of belief in such things as oracles, dreams or prayers. People now do not generally believe that prayers work (but they hope nonetheless). In the modern world it's an easy jump for the Distant Deity to become an equally distant Unifying Principle or Abstract Ideal, one which finds itself more congenial to science and the scientifically objective mind...at the loss of the magic and mystery of a personal God possessing human characteristics, like jealousy, anger, etc...or foreknowledge, creativity and playfulness.

BIRDS OF OMEN

We have mentioned the birds already as harbingers, as the messengers between gods and men. Their realm generally is the field of air between Earth and Heaven, and they are allowed to eavesdrop on conversations between the gods. There are the Egyptian oracle birds, and the Druidic birds of omen up north in the Hyperborean regions. And we have heard from the Aeginetan Corone, and the snow-white bird of Apollo.

Augury as a 'science' or art goes back much farther than the word, but we can see in it the 'v' (there was no 'u' in Latin), as in aviary, avis, etc. This relates to birds, and even the Emperor Augustus borrowed some glory from Roman beginnings when he adopted that name. (It had still perhaps to the Romans of his own time the ring of the ancient chief who was also the keeper of religious lore. Perhaps it is interesting too to note that Octavian had therefore two titles, one civil, one religious.)

In one Egyptian creation story it is a goose that lays the egg from which the world and all the elements are hatched. Ra is identified with the falcon as he rises on the wings of morning, triumphant over the forces of both light and darkness. The ibis as a sacred bird is revered back through unimagined time. The eagle still holds a mystic glamour, as it has through ages as a symbol of power and dominance. It is an eagle that drops the wolf pup into the lap of Claudius, signifying in no uncertain terms his ultimate ascension to the Imperial Throne of Rome.

Augury achieved its pinnacle of art and belief in Rome probably some time before the end of the Republic...Plutarch's era. Little was set down, in those remote and less literate times, and we can only reconstruct in imagination the knowledge which a Tiresias might have owned. The love of interpretation **per se** among the ancients is very evident, and the skill in divining successfully in some consistent fashion would lead to a reputation as a Tiresias or a Daniel. Modern man has little sympathy with interpretation and the uncertain results it yields (unlike his beloved machines which do everything the same way every time without chance and without romance). But results were still important to the ancients, hence the importance of the track record of an oracle such as the Pythoness at Delphi.

The wren, the blackbird, the raven, the crow, the hawk, the owl, the swan and the crane were all magical totems in Druidic belief. We've retained fascination with many of these...the owl as wise, the robin as signifying spring, but the general knowledge of the significance of birds as icons is lost. Poe still thought of the raven, for instance, as prophetic, that its ability to speak made it an even more truthful messenger from oracular realms; but did he know that this bird is also associated with healing? Perhaps he did, for the realization of the truth that is in fact mirrored by knowledge within, and an acceptance of its truth is in itself part of the healing art...psychology.

And if that science, as it might in the ancient world, had a totem of its own, it would surely be the raven.

The raven plies its way between the world and the underworld in ancient lore, and it is its blackness perhaps that lends its being cast upon the dark side, and its perhaps undeserved reputation as a bird of ill omen. Just as Pluto in the ancient world has none or few of the habiliments (bat wings and horns!) or evil traits of Satan in the Judeo-Christian Book. The word 'plutocrat' comes from the idea that Pluto possessed all the riches imaginable, such as gold, diamonds, rubies, emeralds, etc. (all of which come into the world from underground) and he gives them up freely to anyone who digs in the right places. He has plenty and he is a friend to mankind, unlike the sullen and resentful villain of Milton and the Christians.

To the Greeks, Pluto was the lord of his realm, but a host and not a warden. We must remember, that short of apotheosis, no mortal entered into Heaven. Even in the Orphic cults the idea of a blissful paradise was nothing like that of the Christians and later Islam. The afterlife at best was rather shadowy and vague, and the practice of inhumation had its effect on beliefs about a continuing spiritual existence in a shadowy underworld, where the spirit waited for its next birth into the world above, from waiting room to weary wheel.

Birds have always been seen mainly as the connection between Heaven and Earth, and even the Holy Ghost is customarily represented as a dove in Christian iconography…harbinger of grace and peace, again rather too straightforward and simple to an ancient, but then in the modern world much less is left to chance, and of course we too now fly, and have taken the mystery out of most of that. We're more concerned with landing safely than with running into any gods, bumping into Icarus or getting run over by Phaeton. o tempora, o mores!

VII.

THE CHRISTIAN WORLD

NOSTRADAMUS—THE LAST ORACLE?

Belief in the truth and efficacy of oracular utterances was apparently universal before the advent of Christianity, but as the new religion grew and flourished it found it necessary to the health and continuance of its own dogma to relegate  the beliefs of all others to the realm of superstition, heterodoxy or downright heresy. In the course of time the oracular tradition of Greece and Rome was swamped by the universality of Orthodox Christian belief, which led to the claim by the Christians that all oracles became silent precisely at the birth of Jesus. Still the influence of ancient oracles manifests itself in our later cultural history, and the assumption by the poet that the audience knows what an oracle is—however untrustworthy it is taken to be…as with the witches in Shakespeare's *MacBeth*,

> …that palter with us in a double sense
> Act V, scene viii

…or *Julius Caesar*
> Beware the Ides of March.
> Act I, scene ii

and much other popular drama and fiction (we have mentioned Merlin, a figure like these with one foot in history and the other in legend, song and story), indicating that such beliefs persist still among the commonality, many of whom supplement their own most fervent prayers by consulting fortune tellers and astrologers. Prophets of the oracular variety still emerge throughout the history of Europe and the West and still have their influence on people and events. The madman Adolph Hitler, who never made a move without consulting his astrologers and his propagandist Josef Goebels, delved into the prophesies of the 16th Century Frenchman Michael Nostradamus for certain predictions concerning the outcome of World War II. Hitler's propagandist Goebels interpreted some prophesies of the seer which seemed to satisfy the desires of the Germans and Hitler in particular, but the revival of Nostradamus by the Germans prompted the Allies to consult the text as well, and they found much more in the prophetic writings to reassure them of their own ultimate victory.

Remembering Onomacritus of Greece, the 'oracle monger' of Herodotus' *History*, who after being disgraced in Athens for 'editing' or falsifying oracles contained in poems attributed to Musaeus (a disciple of Orpheus) left Athens and joined the court of Xerxes in Persia, again bending oracles to suit occasions and to curry favor with the Great King. Onomacritus was an ancient precursor of Herr Goebels, but the reason it is brought up here is that it points up the fact that oracles were of at least two kinds, those uttered at the instance of the suppliant with direct bearing on the question, and those more general (or vague) as to place and time, that remain to be 'fitted' to future events. These latter are what we shall encounter with the prophesies of Nostradamus.

Unusual as we might find an oracle of such reputation as Nostradamus in the fully Christian Europe of the 16th Century, the belief in such utterances persists, as we say, and the success of his predictions lends credence to the verses he wrote touching on events long after his lifetime.

Jh hoc
signo
vinces.

The Jewish/Christian physician who appears in the middle of plague years and inquisition, surfaces like Aristeas once again, an Orphic in a strange land, whose personal and mortal 'present' is shaky as ashes, who nonetheless travels freely through the time machine of his own quatrains, unable to keep his visions to himself, and knows their worth, even though he may not know just what they mean. Like Plato's poet, proceeding more from inspiration than art or reason.

Michel de Nostradamus, learned doctor of medicine, astrologer, royal advisor and scholar of arcane and occult works, wrote quatrains of verse while in a self-induced trance, without himself always apprehending their meaning. This is very reminiscent of the procedure at Delphi, where the Pythoness, in a trance, sitting on her tripod, spoke a language unintelligible even to her, but known to the priests, who issued her answer in hexametric verse.

Unlike the Delphic Oracle which functioned under the aegis of the god Apollo, Nostradamus, from a family of Christianized Jews, in an age when the infamous Inquisition found itself dangerously nervous about all hint of heresy, was at least protected by the puzzling nature of his metaphorical verse, as well as the fact that it was so subject to interpretation; and the admittedly automatic nature of his inspirations in some sense absolved the good doctor himself from responsibility in the matter. It was still dangerous. He could in that era have been burned at the stake as a witch as well as a heretic, and indeed was called to account by the Inquisition on at least one occasion, for referring to the stone angels being carved for a cathedral as 'devils.' He averred that he was only referring to the quality of the workmanship.

His 'Centuries' (nothing to do with the calendar) are books containing 100 quatrains in each. There are ten 'Centuries.' The quatrain looks like this (translated from French into English):

> Seated at night in my secret study,
> Alone, reposing over the brass tripod,
> A slender flame leaps out of the solitude,
> Making me pronounce that which is not in vain.
>
> C.I, v.1

The verse above is the first quatrain of the first Century. The second continues the description of his method:

> With divining rod in hand, I wet the limb and foot
> Set in the middle of the branches,
> Fearsome awe trembles my hand, I await,
> Heavenly Splendor! The Divine Genius sitteth by.
>
> C.I, v.2

Of the verses thereafter nearly all concern the future. One other notable exception may be found in Nostradamus' incantation:

> Those that read these verses,
> Let them read them with a mature mind,
> Let not the profane, vulgar and ignorant be attracted;
> All astrologers, fools and barbarians keep away.
> Who disobeys is cursed according to rite.

But the verses he sets down have no chronological order, being unconscious and automatic, and each must be deciphered in the light of its own time, place and events. It should be noted again that unlike the Delphic Oracle, Nostradamus in his day had no office, no recognized function in the society. He pursued his mystical prognostications in spite of the accepted and official religion of his time rather than with its sponsorship. No tithes were granted him, although he did gain the attention and approval of the legendary Catherine de Medici, Queen of France and prima arbitrex of custom and style in Europe at the time. The Queen's favor was strong protection. Still, no doubt, Nostradamus felt more security in the metaphorical and puzzling poetry of his quatrains. The fact that his verses did not easily divulge their meaning, and like most oracular utterances had the character of riddles, kept the Inquisition's thought police from the prophet's door. The incantation to read his quatrains with a mature mind is well taken, and of course the prophecies extend far beyond Nostradamus' own time, so that often we find the predicted event but a piece in the jigsaw puzzle of historical fulfillment that may sooner or later fit into the larger picture, and sometimes the verse will fit in its description, again because of its mysterious imagery, with more than one cataclysmic event, as in the one which predicts the coming of Napoleon, but may also refer to Hitler:

> From the deepest part of Western Europe
> From poor people a child will be born
> Who shall seduce many with his words.
> His fame shall increase in the Eastern Kingdom.
> C.III, v.35

Since history often repeats itself there is an added difficulty in many interpretations. This author is of the opinion that the quatrain points directly to Hitler, because of the rather specific reference to the 'Eastern Kingdom' (in German, Osterreich, or Austria, the country of Hitler's birth).

There are many quatrains which seem to refer to Napoleon, and many more that point to Adolph Hitler, both seen as destroyers of mankind, as 'Antichrists.' Another famous leader is mentioned in several places, Elizabeth I of England:

> She who was cast out shall return,
> Her enemies found to be conspirators.
> More than others her Age triumphs,
> At three and seventy to die most surely.
> C.VI, v.74

Of course 'The Elizabethan Age' is still far-famed. Elizabeth died at seventy, but in 1603, so we may have this latitude in our interpretation. Time is a prob-

lem in interpreting Nostradamus. The conjunction of events is sometimes help-
ful, as are the times indicated by astrological (astronomical) conjunctions. And
even in those verses where a year is indicated we have the problem of Nostradamus' habit of dating events from some seemingly arbitrary point, such as
the Council of Nicea in 325 A.D., a date of far less significance to us than to
Nostradamus.

Great historical personages figure prominently in the verses. Hitler, as we have
seen, and Elizabeth I. Napoleon figures prominently as he might, the events of
his career affecting Nostradamus' own country; and there seems something about
charismatic personalities that, like the momentous events they initiate, pierce
more readily through the mystic ether; as for example the Italian leader Mussolini:

> The wild black one, after he shall have tried
> His bloody hand by fire, sword, bended bows,
> All the people shall be so frightened,
> To see the greatest hanged by neck and feet.
>
> C.IV, v.47

Mussolini's fascist party was called 'The Black Shirts,' and his death is fairly
described in the last line, as his corpse and that of his mistress were trussed up
by the feet in the square for the mob to spit on.

Nostradamus' verses seem most specific when dealing with events closest to
his own time and place, as in the following quatrain:

> The Royal infant shall despise his mother,
> Eye, feet wounded, rude, disobedient,
> News to a lady very strange and bitter.
> There shall be killed about five hundred.
>
> C.VII, v.11

In 1615, King Louis XIII of France, then a boy of fifteen, was persuaded to
make war on his mother, Queen Marie, who was at the time Regent. In the
resulting hostilities about five hundred of the Queen's soldiers were killed. Line
two suggests also a (reverse) Oedipal relationship. 'Oedipus' means 'Piercefoot,'
and that royal prince blinded himself in shame in the denouement of Sophocles'
great play.

And as the reader may see by now there is a playfulness about these portents
in poetry, however that often grim humor may have been unintended. Still, riddles are often jokes, jokes often riddles...and we can find that ambiguous wit in

the life of Nostradamus. There is the famous tale of the black pig and the white pig. Invited to dine with a Monsieur Florenville, Nostradamus, being shown two pigs, a black one and a white one, was asked what would become of them. Nostradamus replied that they would eat the black one and the wolf would eat the white one. To trick Nostradamus, and perhaps to show him up as a fraud, the host secretly ordered the cook to prepare the white pig for their supper. At the end of the meal, Florenville asked Nostradamus which pig they had eaten, and Nostradamus repeated his earlier statement, that they had eaten the black pig and the wolf had eaten the white one. The host called the cook in to refute the prophet, and was told by the cook that an accident had occurred...a wolf cub had nibbled on the white pig, so he had served them the black pig instead.

Shades of Croesus and the Pythoness! If there is a moral here, it is that you can't fool the prophet or thwart a prophecy. Nostradamus, if he knew as much as he did about the outcome, must have known that his host would play this game with him. And the presence of the wolf in the prophecy seems like the bait on the hook, or the cheese in the trap that's sure to snap. Chance is virtually ruled out. Florenville should have known better.

We can say that with hindsight at least. The trouble with the quatrains as prophecy is that one may not know how well the prophecy fits until all the events have taken place. So the riddle may be solved too late at least for some. Another cosmic joke? Perhaps. Adolph Hitler was encouraged by certain prophecies, indicating (early) success, only to go on to fulfill the bad end predicted in other quatrains.

> The arm hanging and the leg bound,
> With a pale face, a dagger in the bosom,
> Three shall be sworn to the fray,
> To the great one of Genoa the iron shall be darted.
>
> C.V, v.28

In 1944, Hitler was the object of an assassination attempt by his officers (the 'dagger in the bosom' is reminiscent of Caesar's assassination at the hands of Brutus and the conspirators...the Brutus here being a colonel named Von Staufenberg, who planted the bomb in Hitler's bunker). The Fuehrer was wounded in arm and leg, and thereafter walked with a limp. This was about the time of Mussolini's fall, and signaled the beginning of the end for the three Axis powers.

> He who by iron shall destroy his father, born in Nonnaire.

Shall in the end carry the blood of the Gorgon,
Shall in a strange country make all so silent,
That he shall burn himself, and his double talk.

C.VIII, v.79

Hitler was born Adolph Schickelgruber, and in changing his name denied family and father; yet perhaps 'destroy his father' refers to 'The Fatherland,' as Germany is commonly called by its citizens. "Nonnaire' may be a reference to a nunnery, and that may lead to an interpretation more circumstantial than provable, but which illustrates the kind of fun you can have with The *Centuries*.. Considering that Nostradamus might be employing a witticism or insult perhaps common in the 16th century, which is to say that if you said someone was born in a nunnery, it would be a euphemistic (but clever) way of calling him a bastard. We may get little argument on the point. From Austria, his birthplace, Hitler carried 'the blood of the Gorgon' (which heals on the one hand, destroys on the other) to a strange country (Germany), which after building up, he carried down with him, suppressing all dissent. At the end he ordered his own body to be burned outside the bunker, his deceitful influence dying with him.

One can argue with these interpretations, yet disagreement is the joy of students of Nostradamus. If indeed we find it best to take the verses cum grano salis, they still provide endless entertainment and exercise for our powers of interpretation.

And sometimes the quatrain leaps up and bites your imagination. In January of 1991, while watching television coverage of the progress of the desert war, called 'Desert Storm,' this writer was struck by the strange images of night video recording the flashes and explosions over Baghdad (it looked as surreal as Van Gogh's *Starry Night*). I felt the impulse to consult the prophet to see if there could be any allusion to this great battle, virtually unfolding in real time, like a spectator sport. Turning to Century VI, I found this quatrain:

The sky will burn at 45 degrees,
Fire approaches the great new city.
Immediately a huge, scattered flame leaps up
When they want to have proof of the Normans.

C. VI, v.97

At that moment the Iraqis were sending SCUD missiles against Tel Aviv, and this could well have been what Nostradamus meant by 'Fire approaches the great new city.' Tel Aviv was founded in 1909. The 'scattered flame' leaping up would certainly be Patriot missiles, sent up in defense of the town. By this time, excited at the prospects of the verse, I looked at my world globe, to find 45 degrees longitude running through the suburbs of Baghdad and down to Basra. But is it convincing yet? When the date is not specific, every event has to be nailed down, and Nostradamus, with his usual playfulness, does exactly that. 'When they want to have proof of the Normans.' The Americans kept their promise (with Patriot missiles) to defend Israel, giving that 'proof.' And finally, the General in Chief of the battle was not only a Norman (European, by descent), his name was Norman! Not just Norman but Norman 'S' (Schwarzkopf!)

I was so moved by what seemed the explicit prediction of this verse that I sent a letter off to the general (by this time hostilities had ceased) with my interpretation, and even exercising a bit of temerity, I warned him that history itself works prophetically, in the sense that it tends to repeat. At the Battle of Issus in 330 B.C. Alexander the Great destroyed the army of Darius; but Darius escaped and was able to gather another army, and Alexander had it all to do over again.

We shall see.

> In the year 1999 and seven months
> From the sky will come the Great King of Terror;
> He will revive the Great King of the Mongols.
> Before and after war reigns happily.
>
> C.VI, v.97

A frightening prophecy indeed, because of its specificity, until we consider the prophet's way of counting the years, in which case we have ten or a dozen generations before we have to worry. Still, as I write this (April of 1999) and remembering that 'happily' could be interpreted as 'in a good cause,' we may have begun the prophecy's proving out, as we get set to topple Milosevic and his genocidal friends, hopefully and happily. What happens next, who is the 'Great King of Terror,' and who the 'King of the Mongols,' all these may be answered soon.

VIII.

HOW TO START
YOUR OWN RELIGION

"...the prophetic tablet of the mind has no writing on it..."

THE SPIRIT FREED

And now we seem to have come around again to Plutarch's remark about the "prophetic tablet" and the writing that isn't there. How desperate we writers are for meaningful metaphors! And I mean that with all sincerity. But then he says "…no definition provided by itself" That's where it gets mystical. It's a mental pretzel, an intellectual wake-up call. If you think about it, it looks either like nonsense or the answer to everything we've sought here, or again, perhaps only a Plutarchian joke, something to make us stop and think, for just these few words are enough to stand one's hair on end, particularly in the modern world. If I were quoted these words on the Big Challenge and I didn't know already who wrote them, I'd be forced to guess Anthony Ashley Cooper, John Locke's brilliant but recalcitrant pupil. It was Locke who spoke of the *tabula rasa*, the empty black-board of our mind "upon which experience writes," and it was Locke whose idea fit the template for the age which followed him. Locke's student, Cooper, opposed Locke's view with all his might.

Anthony Ashley Cooper, 3rd Earl of Shaftesbury, held the line for the Platonists in the age of English Empirical philosophy, which explored almost exclusively the kind of pragmatic thinking that seemed necessary to the Industrial Revolution soon to follow: the skepticism of Hume and the Machiavellian politics of Hobbes, the mechanical vision of Bacon, and the empirical view of existence held by Cooper's teacher, Locke, were all instrumental in forging the consensus. Cooper was out in the cold, a revolutionary in reverse it might be said, a super reactionary by virtue of his rather atavistic metaphysics. It was the 3rd Earl…and the Cambridge Platonists…who stopped short of denying to humans a spirit immortal which was capable of understanding implicitly, innately and naturally certain eternal truths; Cooper believed that our essence, in effect, precedes our existence.

To put all of this quite another way. The other philosophers were looking for a something…just as Descartes wasted a lot of time searching for the pineal gland (even giving it a name!) to account for any connection between mind and body, and like the man who looked outside for the watch he lost inside the house because the light was better out there, he met with no success…because it wasn't a gland or anything that might employ or support a mortal metaphor. It's a phenomenon, much more like the Occasionalism of Pere Malebranch, who held the notion that God takes a hand in every action.

At that moment when we have abandoned the present, the empirical, when the mortal part of us no longer exists in our calculations, then we may have that epiphany that the only things worth arguing are the imponderables. But all the invention of language and its pigeon holes of convenience and euphemism fall pitifully short of describing that which every man and woman thinks belongs to him or her: a spiritual identity, indefinable as it may be.

The modern world attests to Cooper's unsuccess at turning British pragmatic and official thinking around, yet without a doubt he impressed some very influential continental philosophers like Immanuel Kant, who carried out many of his ideas. The Sage of Koenigsburg explored the idea of innate knowledge without fear of contradicting himself, and reached discoveries about the universality of knowledge undreamt of by the British philosophers, but as necessary to the science that followed as any of their conclusions.

What, you ask, is the difference between these two conceptions of the mind? The British are hard put to find even a suitable metaphor, but they plunge on anyway. If you make things work, the question 'why?' seems superfluous.

Plutarch's definition is quite different. At least it seems less static than Locke's. It is a recognition of the spiritual side of human nature. "Tablet" is a strange word in either context to use as a metaphor for mind. Ashley Cooper might say that the blackboard is not empty...inscribed upon it (if you will) are innate ideas by which we judge the experience that meets us in life; the good, the beautiful, the ugly and the evil. These innate ideas are universal and their immutability rules the cosmos. For Plutarch the tablet is prophetic. Given all these difficulties in grappling metaphorically with the concept of "mind," we might as well add to the confusion and ask if "prophetic" is only one of mind's attributes. It seems so for Plutarch. And we here throughout have been using mind and spirit interchangeably, mind itself possessing understanding and intelligence through the medium of awareness, and having as well a capacity beyond any present imagining which will be the fulfillment of its spiritual nature.

The war being waged between the material and the spiritual has gone on through the eons and at all levels of thought, philosophical and religious, without any final solution. That may be as natural as anything else, part of the yin and yang of all existence, as the Chinese might see.

Can skepticism then destroy our faith in the existence of spirit or soul? Erasmus of Rotterdam said that he left his skepticism at the door of the church. Seventy years of atheistic Communism, much of it spent vigorously rooting out all traces of the Orthodox past in Russia, failed utterly to destroy the peoples' faith in religion. And to describe adequately seventeenth and eighteenth century British thought one must go back, then step out onto any London street to discover that the average bloke still believed in God and his own immortality, in spite of any common sense, no-nonsense attitude he might wear.

> "Everything intrudes," Cooper wrote, "This is life...recruiting, repairing, feeding, cleansing, purging; aliments, rags, excrements, dregs. Which of all the sensations is it for which life is eligible? Where is the day or hour in which we can say we live upon the present and that our happiness is still not future and in promise? what is it that we call sweet in life?"

It was as true in the 17th century as it as today. It was as true for His Lordship as it was for the man in the street. The office, the trash, the subway, the cash, the kids and the spouse and the unpaid mortgage on the house...spirituality remains submerged by necessity, and Sunday morning isn't long enough to meditate on anything. And if you ask the philosopher about how to free yourself from the world's guff, he's going to tell you, in so many words: "It's your problem."

Of course it isn't easy, necessity presses upon our senses, and the present, the seeming reality of the load we carry, threatens to make us beasts of burden, dumb as the ox...vis-a-vis eternity. Like it or not that's the essence of philosophy. It doesn't hang out a neon sign, and if it does, it's usually a warning: NOT FOR EVERYONE.

The reasoning is this: If you love wisdom, if you seek the good, if you hanker after the things of the spirit, want to know beauty and look for knowledge with understanding...if you love these things, as you want in your poetry, religion and romance to define love as a complete love, a love of God or love of The Good, a love divine and everlasting, love self-sacrificing and unselfish...love is always an affair of the spirit. It's when you leave all else and follow after your vision. You sign up for the duration.

And having done that, you've only stepped out onto the long, uncrowded highway, to thumb your way to a place unknown, like Aristeas, an adventurer of the spirit, against the advice, of course, of family and friends. It is also necessary to declare yourself as "different." Nothing so enrages people as being told that. But it is necessary that you accept your own individuality to understand what is meant by:...no definition provided by itself...The mind is the medium through which we understand, a gift denied to other of God's creatures, for we can imagine eternity, and are capable at least of seeking an understanding of our place in it. For Ashley Cooper, mind is a process...For Plutarch when mind is unencumbered by worldly, material considerations, when it is able to divorce itself from the present, it is capable of a destiny and a reach far greater than that which could be defined (or imagined)—even by itself.

We've used many adjectives in attempting to define spirit, to limn some picture of it, but happily the concept escapes all confining definitions, all retaining parameters. It partakes of the boundless, as Anaximander thought, and it defies fences. The possibilities are endless. It is only our limited view that reduces the soul to anything definable. The spirit is not of this world and is free in its own aspect. It is freedom itself. The stoics knew that. Epictetus the slave knew it. Only his mortality was subject to anything. The early Christians felt it deeply. The Jews, dispersed and in captivity, felt it, knew it, and it sustained them.

Beauty speaks to the courageous; the oracles speak to those who trust in them. We must end as we began, with an open mind and a sympathetic ear, for there is territory yet to be charted, not in ancient worlds only, or distant times, but within ourselves, for all we learn of others tells us of ourselves. As gods now we do go forth in our thinking, for now that we have surveyed what we knew all along...that there is precious little to argue about the details once we have noted all the similarities...that we have the makings of a religion congenial to the human spirit, founded itself on the certainty that there is spirit in the universe, even if it's only us. Whether it was Eros Phanes who started it all, or Kronos and Rhea, or Ahura Mazda, or it was all an accident...we are the beneficiaries. It's ours to do with what we will, and to quibble seriously over the historical details is a waste of time...the damage is done and here we are, and we can't help thinking that we are at least half-divine, like Jesus or Mohammed, travelers through Eternity, sharing in the gift of life, and nothing loth to look too closely at the gift or to ask where it came from, intrepid or impertinent, but human all the same. We are the gods. The Earth is ours. Why argue about the details? Of course even the gods are at odds, for it is in the nature of things that give-and-take is the rule that rules all in the boundless...as Anaximander (again) knew, alee same don Juan Matus in the American desert.

Even as gods we are as subject to that principle as we are to Fate and cruel Time, a violence as easy to understand as the regular irregularities of the lunar tides, as inescapable as the forward march of time, as necessary as conflict, impact, friction, resistance, perturbation, competition, chance and danger are to the idea of survival and life itself,. *vs* for instance some sort of inert state. Our rule here could be that we should take Krishna's advice…life is what it is and what it is is a battlefield…so we accept the gift and the trouble it brings as well. As gods then we create our own religion. All the best have counseled self-awareness, have seen the soul as a spirit in transit, from chaos to some final reward, some Valhalla, perhaps returned at last to the nothing and the nowhere from whence it commenced, finally divested of all illusion all desire, all purpose. This is the fervent hope and faith of many

…-but until then…!

As gods we are obliged to discover what it means to be god-like—to be human. "Know what you are!" should perhaps be the modern rendering of "Know thyself," which like the 'Hail, Mary' has become a thoughtless incantation. "Know what you are!" (to which should be added as well…"and do it without fear!"). Don Juan counsels the mood of a warrior. This for most translates as courage, but it also points to the obligation to acquit oneself with honor, that what we do reflects upon who and what we are. Self-esteem is important to conduct, confidence in one's worth contributes to success.

Xenophon might see it that way, and like him, you may (not realizing that you are a god) wish to know which gods to pray to before you embark on some perilous or uncertain adventure. Socrates thought the form of his former pupil's question as put to the Pythoness was all wrong…that Xenophon should have been more direct and simply ask if he should go at all. Posterity in this case however put the student in the right, for Xenophon prayed to the right gods (and did all the other things he needed to do) and wrote himself into history. What Xenophon and Socrates share in spite of any differences, is the certain knowledge that they have enough religion for their own purposes. It's a god-like view of the self. That's not a license to kill, for Xenophon and Socrates both knew the limits beyond which ambition or pride pollutes the soul, the spirit and the self, how any deed or act may be poisoned by evil intent, and how the purity of geometry, logic and justice are matched…or should be. As gods we take a hand, have an opinion. Still we must practice a cosmopolitan objectivity, an unsneering tolerance, which must accompany such independence.

To put it in plain terms, we are obliged to be what we should have become. That's the prick that spurs all endeavor. We must realize what it means to be human, or try at least, to have life and spirit…or it's wasted. What that means to different people at different times and different places varies as it must, but it is the human answer to the relentless and indifferent give and take of nature and of fate that rules in all times past and future and all possible worlds.

Like gods we have the capacity to grasp eternity, and certain basic truths, both empirically and intuitively...as for example the relationship between music and mathematics, and the truth that while the rules are only coincidental they are always in force when it comes to up and down and two plus two...that is the universal and the abstract. There are no difficult concepts to the intuitive mind freed from the present. Just as we can imagine in silence unheard notes of the sweetest music, we can therefore invent our own mythos, and have done so again and again and again as we see in all the digressive, creative manifestations from Orpheus to the present, the basic strain, the bottom chord, the tonic that returns whatever the variation, the highlights, the melody, in one form or another indispensable...

We war like gods as well, with no advantage clearly gained of good or ill...no closer to the heart's desire at the end than we were at the beginning, in bootless and attritional strife over unimportant details, in sometimes pointless defiance of reason, or in simply asserting human independence. It's the battlefield all right, but it is more than simply a battle between good and evil. It's all gray between that black and white, there in no man's land, and humans being what they are...bless'em...it leads to useless difficulties. So Krishna's observation and advice are well taken. It is what it is. The lesson here might be that the way we feel about anything is of more importance to us than the thing itself. Like love, patriotism or despair.

Don't give in to despair. That could be one of our commandments (recommendations). With the assurance attached that nothing in the universe...whether nuclear or spiritual...is ever lost. That random is an order not yet understood. Even chaos and darkness are necessary as we learn from the study of plant life. The deathless cycle gives its own kind of reassurance of course that there will be some kind of future to predict.

You won't need a church or cathedral. There is no congregation, for you will have no following. It's a bad idea. Those guys had to be saints, like Socrates and Jesus, to put up with having people following them around, taking down everything they had to say. And you damn well know they're going to get it wrong, no matter how bright its beginning, and you'll end up saying: "That's not it. That's not what I meant at all."

There are no commandments, no priests, no rabbis in our religion. If a guide is needed he can be sought, but not idolized. Respect for one's teacher is only logical. Even payment is okay. Socrates would never take money for his instruction. He believed as I do that knowledge is not a commodity. My view is this: knowledge is many things. We have mentioned fire. Like fire knowledge may be transmitted with no loss to itself. And the water man who trudges up from the well to sell his water, is not really selling water but is providing a service. To those who complain that water is free he need only reply: "Then go down and get your own." He understands as they seem not to, that a person is worth the labor and that service too, is as negotiable as currency. So in our religion it is all right to take payment for instruction, for, commodity or not, free or not, knowledge is our quest and our reward, and he or she who brings it to us, shares it, is more than worthy of respect.

In my version, all institutions would be suspect and avoided, as being naturally antagonistic toward all creativity and individuality, including all the presently popular churches and religions, those of 'learning' as well.

Like Jesus, Socrates never wrote anything down; like Jesus, Socrates was an example of Orphic spirituality and understood the connection between the universal and the specific, both realized the link between their thinking and the cosmos, the eternal in the abstract, the very divinity of thought, understood the Pythagorean design implicit in its abstract truth; everything we know about either affirms the Orphic immortality of all of us in spirit. Old man Blake was wrong about Newton, when he complained that the noted mathematician had reduced the universe to a heap of sand. There's beauty in logic, and in mathematics too, Pythagoras saw the beauty, and so did Galileo. And heard its music.

We need follow no one. We have enough religion for our own purposes, no reason to follow anyone into the jungle, or think you can hitch a ride on a comet. That ain't what we're talking about here. We're talking about humanity, and also the divinity of the human spirit. Each individual is as divine as any priest or king, pope or saint. We need only learn to be our own person to become acquainted with the mysteries. That is the willingness to commune with something good and fine, like a perfect equation, or a piece of music recalled—"...to think immortal thoughts is to partake of immortality." And so I believe too, a renegade catholic who misses the aesthetics of the mass, that beauty enhances goodness, even if it is not dependent upon it!

Don't mouth words! Don't follow wizards. I'm sure that when Jesus returned Orphic-like after all those wandering years, back to his native land, he was embarrassed at being followed around everywhere, and maybe the thought occurred to him: "I'd forgotten just how God-mad these people are!" He must

have smelt trouble from the first. It is a deplorable trait humans have of following, yet maybe worse than that is their habit of placing all the responsibility on
a scapegoat.

Take responsibility for yourself; it is useless to keep scores and hold grudges.
Forgiveness goes hand in hand with tolerance. Commune then with good. Inves-
tigate the advantages of not taking the world too seriously. It is a very small place
and is not getting any bigger. A good humor should be the goal of any philosophy, as Confucius or someone said. Spiritual communion may consist of something no more important than reading a poem, diving into a Van Gogh, or
taking a stroll through a museum. Many people think of museums as if they were
mausoleums...nothing is further from the truth or any intent. Museums make
great art accessible to everyone. More than losing prejudices, one should
approach the place as a shrine of the spirit, as devout, as sacred as church as a
place of worship (if you will), for when one looks upon beauty, one sees as with
the eye of god gazing upon his own creations...an entirely spiritual notion, to be
sure. I've been to school, but I still don't know how it's done, or even recognized,
but it's intuitive and metaphysical, art strikes the eye or the ear or the reason, but
it's beyond touching because it's all in the mind! It's philosophical and it's religious. It's aesthetic! Pythagoras thought so, and he knew even then that the world
is round. There is no difference between philosophy and religion, as Confucius
knew, and St Augustine too. It hits you in the faith, as Luther might say. And you
go from there.

I'm preaching a new kind of doctrine. It's the only one consistent with any
philosophy of individuality as manifest in spirit...faith in yourself. Don't follow
anyone. It's a contradiction if you do. Philosophies aren't going begging these
days. It's the people who are begging to be shown the way, in religion and in philosophy and they are so in need that they can be taken advantage of by genuine
demons. My message to one and all: Be yourself. It cures drunkenness, recidi-
vism, dope taking, all kinds craziness that lands you up in jail so take it from
someone whose been there and done that, it cures all of that, the lying and the
thieving and the breaches of trust that make you guilty but unrepentant. My cure
does all of that—providing, like Xenophon, you do all the other things you need
to do. Where we're going is more important than where we've been, and the only
things we take with us are those we've given away.

Someone just walked in and threw a net over me {so this thing would get pub-
lished some time}, so I better finish as best I can with all my fingers poking
through this web. Let me just say: the belief in spirit is still with us, even if ora-

cles seem silent. Everything, we find in looking at history, goes around and comes around, and goes around and comes around again. Indeed, after the age of science has lifted us above survival, and we've come to grips with world-wide famine and disease, after the nuclear age has solved all our practical problems, after we have discovered all the possible new worlds, we may at last be blessed with the leisure and the long life conducive to an age of real exploration, an age in which we discover who and what we are, and at last carry out the injunction of the oracle:

KNOW THYSELF.

NOTES BY THE WAY

I think I failed to mention Apuleius' *Golden Ass*. Orphic to the bone, Apuleius comes in rather late on the Orphic scene in the 2nd C A.D.. In his book, Apuleius makes an ass of himself (literally), and the fun begins. Transformation is typical of Orphic tales; metempsychosis is ever kept in mind. And many later Orphic tales, like Finegan's Wake—James Joyce's single-sentence book about the hod carrier who gets bopped on the head with a brick and his friends and family think he's dead. At his wake Finegan does just that and joins the party. Other great works owe their origins to this second century writer, descended by the way from Plutarch, on his mother's side.

Orphic tales and even historical events are often treated and perhaps lived in an Orphic style , intuitively, like Audie Murphy, who goes *To Hell and Back*, writes his own book (like Xenophon), and after being a hero he becomes an actor, which is not surprising at all.

Apuleius belonged to several mystery religions at once, not uncommon in his day, and in using Orphic ideas by the cartload in his travels both as man and ass—and as writer—he is playing to an audience conversant enough with Orphism to 'get' the jokes, and his surrealistic (if you will) parody of its conventions, which by then are generally beyond any mystery to his audience.

The word 'intolerance' is not pejorative. It is merely an observation.

Perhaps a word or two before we go, about Emanuel Swedenborg (1688-1772.) His life is rather different. His visions are not all oracular, but, like Benjamin Franklin, Edison and many others, he was nonetheless gifted with glimpses of the future. Like Alexander at least these gentlemen thought of it first, thus giving proof they could prefigure the ascension of certain ideas or groups of ideas. Swedenborg also saw angels (Cf. Plutarch's Daimonion.) In fact, he claimed that he was visited daily by angels. Now this is not someone given to lying or fantasizing. His name was originally Swedborg. The name Swedenborg was conferred on him by the King of Sweden, as a title of special respect, not only for his theological writings, but also for his contributions in science. He spoke six languages fluently. He improved on the ear trumpet, and invented a device that was the forerunner of our phonograph. He designed a machine gun, was a clock maker and bookbinder. He anticipated Einstein's doctrines on energy. He helped found a science of geology, did extensive work on metallurgy, and even invented a stove, like his American contemporary, Ben Franklin. It was an age with one foot in the future and the other in the past, now moving forward into a world full of scientific wonders, mechanical marvels and a new understanding of the world. And some could see it shaping up before it happened.

By the way, Nostradamus was a plague doctor, sent to trouble spots, because his patients mostly survived. One aspect of his cure was the collecting of rose hips which were dried and ground into a tea, then served to his patients. How did he know about the benefits of vitamin C? So too Swedenborg was possessed of a far-sighted eye. He made the first sketch of a glider, and discovered the circulation and use of cerebral spinal fluid.

Swedenborg predicted the day of his own death, his journey "to the land of the spirits," as he called the after life. He taught that there is a real world which is not in time and space. He thought our material bodies only images of the soul. He was then a Platonist, like Anthony Ashley Cooper.

Swedenborg was hugely admired by William Blake, who, interestingly, saw angels too, and invented a Heaven of his own.

BIBLIOGRAPHY

The following is not a formal bibliography, but a recommendation for reading addressed to those who would like to know more about the topics we have explored.

Anonymous, *Bhagavad Gita*
Anonymous, *The Bible*
Apuleius, Lucius, *The Golden Ass*
Aristotle, *Metaphysics*
Breasted, James Henry, *The Conquest of Civilization*
Bullfinch, *Mythology*
Burnet, John, *Early Greek Philosophy*
Bury, J.B., *A History of Greece.*
Campbell, Joseph, *The Hero with a Thousand Faces*
Ceram, C.W., *Gods, Graves and Scholars*
Dante, *The Divine Comedy*
Durant, Will, *Our Oriental Heritage*
Graf, Fritz, *Greek Mythology–An Introduction*
Graves, Robert, *The Greek Myths*
Graves, Robert, *I, Claudius*
Habicht, Christian, *Pausannias' Guide to Ancient Greece*
Hamilton, Edith, *Mythology*
Harvey, Sir Paul, *Oxford Companion to Classical Literature*
Herodotus, *History*
Hesiod, *Works and Days*
Homer, *Iliad*
Homer, *Odyssey*
Jaeger, Werner, *Paidea*
Kerenyi, C., *The Gods of the Greeks*
Lewis, Neville, *Delphi and the Sacred Way*
London, Jack, *The Star Rover*
MacKendrick, Paul, *The Greek Stones Speak*
Murray, Gilbert, *5 Stages of Greek Religion*

Murray, Gilbert, *The Rise of the Greek Epic*
Nahm, Milton C., *Selections from Early Greek Philosophy*
Nostradamus, Michel de, *Centuries*
Ovid, *Metamorphoses*
Perowne, Stewart, *Roman Mythology*
Petronius Arbiter, *The Satyricon*
Pindar, *Odes*
Plato, 'Timaeus,' 'Cratylus', *Republic, etc.*
Plutarch, *Selected Essays and Dialogues*
Plutarch, *Lives of 12 Noble Greeks and Romans*
Russell, Lord Bertrand, *A History of Philosophy*
Sophocles, *The Theban Plays*
Suetonius, *Lives of the 12 Caesars*
Thucydides, *A History of the Peloponnesian Wars*
Virgil, *Aeneid*
Wells, H.G., *The Outline of History*
Xenophon, *Anabasis, or The March Upcountry*
Xenophon, *A History of My Times*

INDEX

Achaians, 58

Achilles, 60, 71

Acrisius, 53

Adonis, 44

Adrastus, 72

Aeneas, 10, 77, 79

Agamedes, 74

Agamemnon, 71

Ahura Mazda, 41, 45, 100

Alexander the Great, 94

Altamira, 62

Amazons, 31

Amphiaraus, 72

Anabasis, 57, 110

Anaximander, 100

Anchises, 79

Aphrodite, 33

Apis, 76

Apolline, 34

Apollo, 28, 36, 58-59, 61-62, 71, 73-74, 79, 81, 89

Aramaic, 6

Arcadia, 7, 43

Ares, 64-66

Argo, 26, 29

Argonauts, 25, 28

Argosy, 56

Arismapeia, 35

Aristeas, 35-36, 88, 99

Aristodemus, 70

Aristotle, 8, 10, 18, 54, 109

Arjuna, 47-48

Artemis, 73

Asclepius, 73
Athena, 31, 65, 68-69
Athens, 7-8, 11, 21, 30, 33, 41-42, 63, 66, 74, 76, 88
atomic theory, 8, 10
Attica, 42
Attis, 44
Augury, 60, 82
Axis Powers, 92

Baal, 43
Babylon, 11, 53
Bacis, 64
Baghavad Gita, 1
Baghdad, 93-94
bakkid, 55
Balder, 44
Baptist, 17
Barbarians, 64, 89
Barbaroi, 58
Basra, 94
Bastogne, 58
Belshazar, 54
Berkeley, 18
Bible, 30, 55, 109
Birds of omen, 81
Bismark, 17
Boetia, 76
Book of Humanity, 44
Brahma, 43
Brahmins, 37
Brilliance, 63
Brutus, 92
Buddha, 29, 46-48
Buddhism, 46
Byzantium, 69

Calchas, 71-72

Caligula, 80
Calliope, 28
Cambyses, 68
Carthage, 5
Cassandra, 55
Catherine de Medici, 90
Catholic, 103
Cecrops, 65
Centuries, The, 6, 89
Cerberus, 28
Chaos, 13, 101-102
Charon, 28
China, 11
Christianity, 17, 43, 45-46, 80-81, 87
Cleomenes, 67
Colchis, 5
Constantinople, 69
Coretas, 62
Coronis, 73
Cratylus, 30, 110
Crete, 5-6
Crisa, 63
Croesus, 66-67, 92
Cronides, 66
Crotona, 41-42
Cumae, 79-80
Cynicism, 43
Cyrus, 57

Danae, 53
Daniel, 54, 82
Darius I, 46
Daunia, 72
Delians, 74
Delos, 74
Delphi, 14, 36, 55, 61-65, 68-74, 79, 82, 88, 109
Delphic, 21, 62, 64, 66-68, 71, 89-90

Delphyne, 61
Demeter, 31
Democritus, 8, 10
Descartes, 18, 97
Desert Storm, 80, 93
Dionysiac, 33-35, 44
Dionysus, 27, 31, 34
Doriscus, 25

Ecbatana, 68
Egypt, 5-6, 9, 46, 76
Einstein, 13, 107
Elean, 70
Eleusinian, 14, 25, 31
Elis, 63
Elizabeth I, 90-91
Elizabethan Age, 90
Empedocles, 8, 23, 29-30, 33
Epicurean, 19
Epicureans, 36
Europe, 5, 87-88, 90
Eurydice, 26, 28-29

Five Stages of Greek Religion, 42
Fortuna, 80
Freud, 61

Galilee, 14
Geia, 13
Geoffrey of Monmouth, 80
German, 18, 90
Gita, 1, 47-48, 109
Gordius, 60
Gorgon, 53, 92-93
Graces, 63
Graves, Robert, 109

Greece, 5-7, 11-12, 14, 25, 30-32, 35, 37, 41-42, 46, 53-55, 57, 62, 64, 66-
      67, 87-88, 109
Greek, 5-7, 9, 18, 30-33, 35-36, 41-43, 45, 54-55, 57-60, 62-63, 68-69, 72,
      74, 76, 79-80, 109-110
Grove of Argus, 68

Hades, 13, 28, 31, 34
Hamlet, 20, 54, 61
Heaven, 9, 19, 27, 32, 34-36, 41, 46-47, 53, 60, 81, 83, 108
Hebrus, 25
Hell, 9, 46, 107
Hellene, 6
Hellenic, 6, 33, 44
Hellenism, 34
Hellespont, 5
Hera, 61
Heraclitus, 29-30
Hermes, 73
Herodotus, 9, 12, 35, 62, 66, 88, 109
Hesiod, 6, 55, 109
Hippolyta, 31
Holy Ghost, 83
Homer, 6, 31, 55, 58-59, 61, 79, 109
Horus, 43
Hubris, 61
Husayn, 44
Hybris, 66

I Ching, 69
Ilium, 6, 60
Indus Valley, 11
Inquisition, 88-90
Iraqis, 93
Ischys, 73
Isis, 32, 43
Islam, 17-18, 43, 45, 55, 83
Istanbul, 69

Italy, 5-6, 36

Jaeger,Werner, 109
Jason, 25, 28-29, 33, 56
Jeremiah, 44
Jerusalem, 6, 17, 26, 46, 53
Jesus, 17, 29, 42, 44-48, 87, 100, 102-103
Jews, 17, 60, 89, 100
Job, 10, 35, 56
Jocasta, 54, 61
Joy, 63, 93
Judaism, 43, 45-46, 55

Kali, 43
Krishna, 29, 43, 45-48, 101-102

Laius, 54
Lapiths, 73
Last Year at Marienbad, 29
Latium, 77
Leto, 61
Lives of the Twelve Caesars, 80
Livia, 80
Lucretius, 19

Macedonia, 11, 25
Maenads, 27, 29, 34
Magi, 42, 46
Mallus, 72
Mani, 29, 44
Manicheism, 44
Manto, 71, 76
Mardonius, 71
Marseilles, 5
Medes, 60, 64
Media, 41, 46, 63, 68
Mediterranean, 4-6, 10-12

Medusa, 53
Metapontines, 36
Metempsychosis, 44, 107
Milesian, 5
Mithra, 29, 43
Mithraic, 32
Monteverdi, 29, 39
Mopsus, 71-72
Muhammed, 29
Murray, Gilbert, 109-110
Muses, 28
Mussolini, 91-92
Myrmidons, 71
Mysteries, 14, 21, 25, 30-32, 34-36, 41-43, 46, 103

Neoptolemus, 71
Nero, 80
Nomius, 25-28
Nostradamus, Michel de, 110

Octavian, 82
Odessa, 5
Odyssey, 79, 109
Oedipus, 35, 53-55, 61, 91
Oedipus Rex, 35, 54-55
Olympus, 13, 65
Omens, 7, 53, 60
Omphalos, 62
Onomacritus, 33, 88
Orfeo, 29
Oropus, 72
Orpheus, 12, 14, 21, 25-30, 33-37, 41-46, 48, 88, 102
Orphic, 14, 21, 23, 25, 27, 29-37, 39, 41-49, 55, 73, 76, 83, 88, 103, 107
Osiris, 43

Pagan, 19, 45, 79
Paidea, 109

Pan, 61, 79

Parnassus, 62-63

Pausanias, 53

Peloponnesian, 57, 110

Pentateuch, 55

Peripatetic, 12

Persephone, 31

Persepolis, 46

Perseus, 53

Persian, 11, 42, 57, 66, 70

Petronius Arbiter, 80, 110

Phaedrus, 20

Philip, 25

Philomelus, 68

Phlegyas, 73

Phocian, 68

Phoenicians, 5-6, 11

Pindar, 55, 110

Pisistratus, 33, 41-42

Platea, 53, 70-71

Plato, 7-8, 10, 12, 18, 20-21, 29, 42, 45, 57, 88, 110

Plutarch, 20-21, 29, 57, 62, 75, 82, 97-98, 100, 107, 110

Pluto, 28-29, 31, 83

Polonius, 61

Praeneste, 80

Priam, 60

Proconnesus, 35

Prometheus, 27

Ptoion, 76

Purifications , Empedocles, 23, 30

Pythagoras, 10, 12, 41-42, 45, 103-104

Pythia, 36, 68-70, 76

Pythians, 70

Python, 28, 61

Pythoness, 55, 62, 64-71, 74, 82, 88, 92, 101

Ra, 82

Reincarnation, 13, 19, 32, 36, 46
Rhea, 13, 100
Roman, 10, 80, 82, 110
Rome, 79-80, 82, 87

Sadyattes, 68
Salamis, 65-66
Samos, 41
Santayana, 43
Satan, 29, 45, 83
Satyricon, 80, 110
Sayings of Jesus, St Thomas, 48
Serapis, 32
Seven Against Thebes, 72
Shakespeare, 20-21, 28, 87
Shaw, 29
Sibyl, 55, 79-80
Sicilian Wars, 68
Sicily, 5-6, 68
Sifting Bridge, 46
Socrates, 7, 20, 30, 45, 57, 60, 73, 75-76, 101-103
Solon, 10, 12
Sophocles, 53-55, 61, 91, 110
Sparta, 7, 63, 67-68, 70
Spartan, 53, 58, 67, 70-71, 74
Spartan General, 53
Spartans, 8, 57-58, 63, 68, 70-71
St. Thomas, 48
Starry Night, 93
Stoicism, 43
Stonehenge, 62
Suetonius, 110
Syracuse, 42, 69
Syria, 68

Tammuz, 44
Tarquinius Superbus, 79

Tartarus, 73
Tegyrae, 74
Tel Aviv, 93
Thales, 10
Theban, 53, 110
Thebes, 53, 63, 72
Themistocles, 66
Thera, 69
Theseus, 31
Thetis, 60
Thrace, 25, 28, 33-34, 44
Thracian, 25, 30, 34, 46
Timarchus, 75-76
Timoleon, 68-69
Tiresias, 53-55, 71, 76, 82
Tisamenes, 70
Titanic, 35
Titans, 34, 45, 48
Toynbee, 44
Transmigration, 13, 26, 44, 46
Tritogeneia, 65
Trophonius, 74-75
Troy, 6, 59, 71, 80

Underworld, 12, 26, 28-29, 35, 41, 79, 83
Utopian, 7

Valhalla, 19, 101
Vatican, 17
Virgil, 29, 77, 79, 110
Vishnu, 43

Wells, H. G., 110

Xerxes, 54, 88

Zagreus, 27, 44

Zarathustra, 29, 41-42, 44-47
Zend Avesta, 41
Zeus, 31, 34, 58-59, 61-62, 65-66, 73
Zionist, 17

www.ingramcontent.com/pod-product-compliance
Lightning Source LLC
Chambersburg PA
CBHW031121180526
45160CB00005B/48/J